HARRIER

Modern Combat Aircraft 13

HARRIER

Bill Gunston

LONDON
IAN ALLAN LTD

Contents

First published 1981
Second revised edition 1984

ISBN 0 7110 1359 4

Published by Ian Allan Ltd, Shepperton, Surrey, and printed by Ian Allan Printing Ltd at their works at Coombelands in Runnymede, England.

Front cover: Harrier GR.3s of No 4 Sqn, RAF Gütersloh./*Barry Ellson – RAF Germany/PR*

Back cover top: Top scorer among Sea Harriers assigned to operation Corporate was XZ457 of 899 Naval Air Squadron (NAS), whose peacetime Modex number 104 was abbreviated to 14 during the hasty hand-painting in dark sea grey with B-type roundels on the voyage south. Further details are given in another caption./*BAe*

Back cover, bottom: This air-to-air portrait of the third YAV-8B aircraft shows clearly that the raised canopy and frameless clear-view windshield are quite different from the raised canopy and three-panel windshield of the Sea Harrier./*MCAir*

Title page: Harrier GR.3 fitted with long range fuel tanks./*MoD*

Introduction

When man first tried to fly he copied the birds. Birds fly by flapping their wings, and in most species this gives them VTOL (vertical take-off and landing) capability. Only a few birds, such as ducks and swans whose wing loading is high, need to accelerate forwards before they can become airborne. It so happens that attempts at human flight by flapping wings have universally been unsuccessful. No flying machine took the air until lift and propulsion were separated, the one being provided by fixed wings and the other by a propeller or other thrusting device. This meant that all man's early flying machines had to race across the surface of our planet in order to reach flying speed. And if they flew too slowly they stalled and fell.

The aircraft described in this book is unique. By the seemingly simple process of vectored thrust (which is explained in the first chapter) it can take-off vertically, hover in the air, fly backwards or sideways, and land vertically. So can helicopters; but the Harrier can also make a running take-off burdened with a much heavier useful load, accelerate forwards over a sloping ramp that catapults it high into the air, fly at supersonic speed, and make 'unbelievable' flight manoeuvres using viffing (vectoring in forward flight) so that the engine thrust pushes it round sharp corners. No helicopter can do this, and, so far as we know in the West, neither can any other of man's flying machines.

I doubt if there is anyone remotely interested in aviation who is not broadly familiar with what a Harrier can do. Millions have watched the strange birds perform at air shows. But in 20 years the number sold has been trivial: for example, about 100 for the RAF and about 100 for the US Marines. One is left with two conclusions: either jet V/STOL (vertical or short takeoff and landing) is not worth having, or the world's air forces have got it wrong. And there is not the slightest doubt it is the second conclusion that is correct.

What is wrong with air forces? Why is it that most of the global interest in the Harrier has come from navies? It is simply that – except in the really professional countries, such as the Soviet Union – armed forces only play at war, but plan for peace. Navies can usefully deploy jet V/STOLs aboard smaller and simpler ships, and as they can do this and save money in peacetime it makes sense and they visit Kingston to talk about Harriers or Sea Harriers. But air forces have nice big airfields, with a long concrete runway. They have no need of a V/STOL. A few are prepared to concede that, one day (never this week!), their nice runway might be bombed. An even smaller number practice shovelling dirt into craters and draw lines with rulers on aerial photographs to prove to their own satisfaction that they could 'take off between the craters'. The thought that their aircraft, and possibly the whole base, might be destroyed in a split second is something they do not wish to discuss, because to this they have no answer.

Several times I have asked NATO base commanders whether they are worried that, without the slightest warning, their base might be hit by a Russian nuclear missile. The exact position of every important military airbase in Western Europe, and almost everywhere in the world, is impossible to hide; and the Russians have enough firepower to take care of the whole lot with missiles to spare. The general answer is 'Oh no! That just could not happen, except in wartime.' The inference is, first, that Western commanders ignore the strong probability that this is how any European war would *begin,* and, second, that Western air forces are not intended for warfare. If they were, they would be equipped with aircraft that can be hidden in places so obscure and numerous that it would not be worth trying to hit them.

New ideas take a long time to be accepted. For at least the first ten years it was fashionable to deride the vectored-thrust V/STOL by repeating parrot-like clichés which revolved around the belief it must suffer severe penalties, or have an oversized engine, or be unable to fly far, or carry a useful load. Only very gradually has the truth become accepted by minds that were all but closed. The truth is that in military aviation vectored thrust is as fundamentally important as the wing. The Harrier was the pioneer, and the starting-point for the future.

Haslemere, England, 1981 *Bill Gunston*

1 Vectored Thrust

Triggered by the Berlin blockade and other hostile acts by the Soviet Union, the nations of Western Europe and North America formed the North Atlantic Treaty Organization (NATO) in 1949. A year later the North Koreans invaded South Korea, plunging many nations into war, a mere five years after World War 2. After a seemingly brief spell of reduced defence budgets, the Free World realised it had to protect itself, and great efforts were made to re-arm and make up for lost time.

Helped enormously by generous funding from the United States, the European NATO countries expanded their output of military aircraft, and also constructed the largest-ever peacetime military infrastructure – a word, typical of the proliferating military jargon of the Americans, meaning fixed installations such as airfields, base depots and fuel pipelines. There were plenty of military airfields already in Western Europe, but they were of wartime size and layout, and scattered right up to the Iron Curtain. They were pleasant places – Fassberg, Wunstorf, Celle, Bückeburg and Fürstenfeldbrück, for example – but it did not need much though to appreciate that in the event of the Warsaw Pact armies rolling westwards these bases would be overrun in hours. So the equivalent of well over £1,000million in today's money was spent in creating a belt of modern airfields much further west, along the approximate line of Germany's western frontier.

These lacked the mature character of the old airfields, for they were made of prefabricated concrete, steel and aluminium. They had a single runway 8,200-12,000ft long, a slim 'tower' on the American plan housing electronics supplied by US companies, and armies of yellow earthmovers churning a landscape of mud. From the air they formed an impressive sight. The white runways stood out from 30 or 40 miles away, often not much more than their own length apart. The new NATO 'basic operating platforms' were hailed as real airpower, on to which were flown the F-84s, F-86s, Hunters, Mystères and other modern warplanes.

Nobody could deny that these were superior bases for modern jets. On a hot day a heavily loaded F-84G could barely use the old wartime fields, where at such places as Bitburg, Spangdahlem, Zweibrücken and Gros Tenquin there was a mile of concrete to spare. When the first supersonic fighters arrived – the first F-100C slammed on to the concrete at Bitburg on 12 March 1956 – there was no problem. NATO's air forces had come a long way since 1949, and were well satisfied with the results.

A week before the first F-100 arrived at Bitburg an elderly Frenchman had climbed the steps to the French Air Ministry in Paris. He was Michel Wibault, once a famous aircraft designer whose metal monoplane fighters had been every bit as advanced in their day as the F-100. In his brief-case were plans for a new kind of fighter of novel design. He was not one of the unceasing army of nut-cases who continually bombard defence staffs with proposals for fantastic but impractical weapons. His ideas were worth more than the usual polite letter expressing regret. But on this occasion he seemed to have something a bit 'far out'.

He called it *Le Gyroptère*. It was a small aircraft for combat purposes – Wibault was not too specific on whether it was a fighter or a ground-attack platform – with a totally new kind of power-plant giving it VTOL (vertical take-off and landing) capability.

The *Gyroptère* was far from being the first proposed VTOL combat aircraft. In the early 1930s pilots of powerful lightweight biplane interceptors had found they could 'hang on the propeller' nose-upwards, at below the rated full-throttle height for the engine – though at speeds so low that they lost aileron control and rotated in the opposite direction to the propeller. In 1944 the Luftwaffe actually flew prototypes of the Ba349 Natter, a rocket interceptor that was launched almost vertically, and thus did not need an airfield. At the same time the Focke-Wulf company completed preliminary studies for a VTOL fighter intended to stand on its tail and screw itself into the air like a helicopter using three *Triebflugel* (thrust-wing) lift/propulsion systems. The *Triebflugel* was a wing with a ramjet or turbojet on its tip, mounted on a free-running ring round the mid-fuselage. Using Pabst ramjets the fighter was calculated to reach 621mph and climb to over 26,000ft in 100 seconds, then pushing over with its tail controls into normal horizontal flight and destroying opponents with four heavy cannon. After the war the US Navy had picked up the idea, but preferred to use nose contraprops driven by the 5,500shp Allison XT40 turboprop. The Lockheed XFV-1 and Convair XFY-1 were extensively tested in an effort to find a VTOL

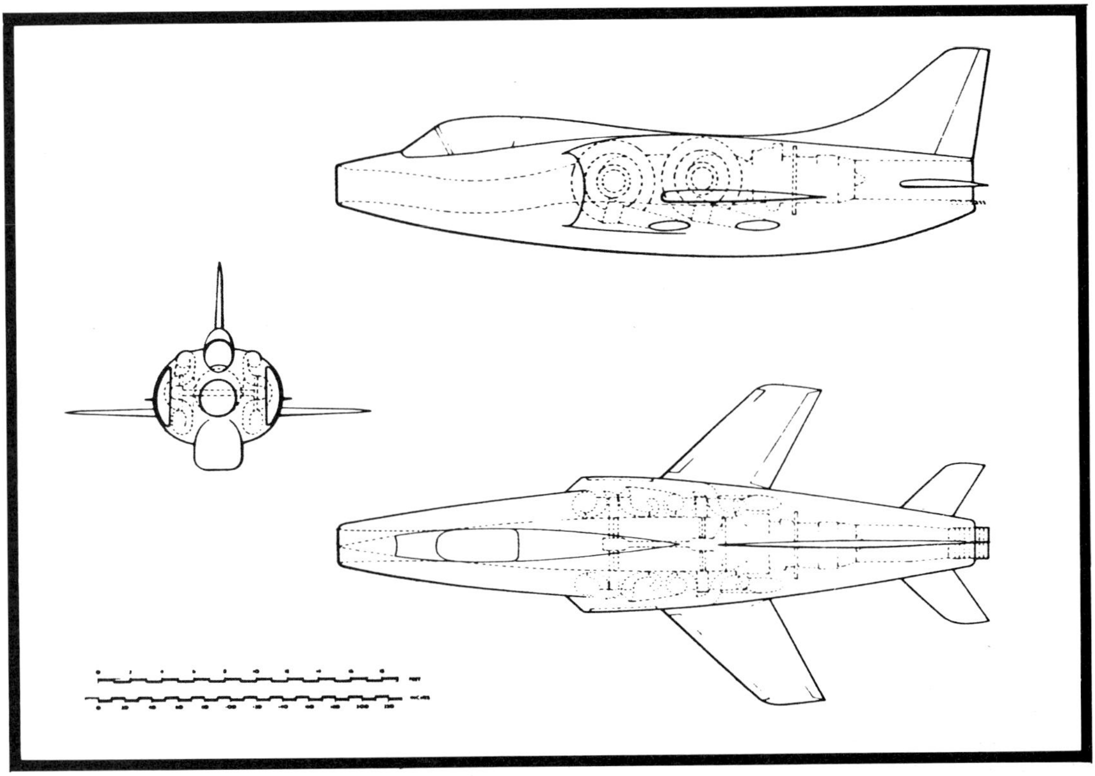

Above: The Wibault Gyroptère was a bold and original concept, but militarily unattractive and technically inefficient./BAe

fighter that could operate from the decks of ordinary ships.

Wibault rightly judged all tail-sitters difficult to fly and hazardous. Even the eminently simple Ryan X-13 Vertijet, which was just a small delta aircraft whose Rolls-Royce Avon turbojet put out more thrust at low altitudes than the gross weight, did not appear to offer the basis for a practical combat aircraft. Bell seemed to be on to a better idea with swivelling or vectored thrust. The original Bell VTO of 1954 had been thrown together from bits of other aircraft, and its two J44 turbojets could be pivoted through 90° to lift it off the ground. Bell's next VTOL aircraft, the X-14, had two Viper turbojets with tail-pipe deflectors under the cg (centre of gravity) of the aircraft to angle the jets vertically down when in the jet-supported VTO mode. Rolls-Royce were extensively researching the whole problem, initially with a 'Flying Bedstead' with two turbojets end-to-end with 90° angled jetpipes, and proposed to promote jet lift using batteries of very light purpose-designed lift jets – possibly several dozen in each aircraft! In Wibault's own country SNECMA was flying an Atar turbojet mounted vertically with landing gear and pilot seat, preparatory to building Count Zborowski's annular-wing *Coléoptère* VTOL fighter – but that was to be another tail-sitter. Wibault believed in the flat-riser.

The purpose behind many of these VTOL schemes was simply that the technology of the gas turbine had made them available and capable of realisation. In Rolls-Royce's case it was the scent of money: several dozen engines per aircraft sounded good for business, even if individually the engines were simple and cheap. But Wibault was motivated by the nagging belief that NATO's splendid infrastructure of runways, hangars, maintenance stores and jet-fuel pipelines could all go up in fireballs in the first few seconds of a European war. He had discussed the matter with generals and politicians, and though all understood and appreciated the problem, none had an answer. It appeared that modern combat aircraft needed two miles of concrete.

Hence the French designer's curious *Gyroptère*, which was lifted off the ground by four nozzles evenly disposed around the cg. They were not turbojets but nozzles for cold air blown out by four large centrifugal compressors. Around each compressor was a rotating scroll, whose exit pipe terminated in the thrust nozzle. When the four scrolls were rotated through 90° the exit pipes lay horizontal under the belly of the aircraft, giving forward thrust. Wibault naturally chose the most powerful engine available to drive the four compressors and selected the Bristol BE.25 Orion turboprop, which though normally flat-rated at below 5,000shp actually generated a sea-level thermodynamic power of over 8,000shp. This sufficed for a total vectored-thrust (lift/thrust) installation suitable for a *Gyroptère* able to fly useful combat missions – though it had no chance of being supersonic.

Wibault visited various groups of officials and found that his best bet was the American-funded MWDP (Mutual Weapons Development Program) and NATO's own Agard (Advisory Group for Aeronautical Research and Development). Col Willis Chapman of MWDP had the Wibault scheme fully evaluated. Nobody could refute the idea, nor the urgent need for it; but nobody liked the engineering. The great Theo von Kármán of Agard was instantly captivated by the fundamental concept. 'Ah,' he said,

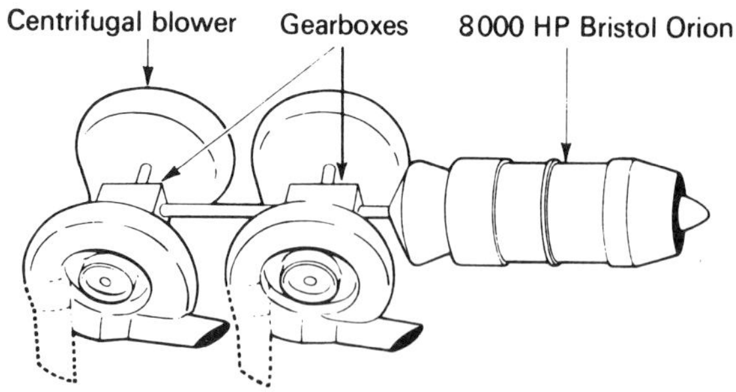

Above right: Wibault's proposal was to use a powerful gas turbine to drive four high-capacity blowers discharging through scrolls which could be vectored to give lift or thrust./*Rolls-Royce*

PERFORMANCE AND AERODYNAMICS DEPARTMENT — 2nd August, 1956

G.N. 1636

To: Dr. Hooker

GYROPTER PROJECT

A brief study of the Wibault report entitled "Ground Attack Gyropter" indicates that the weight assumed for 4 large centrifugal compressors and bevel drive gear boxes (1080 lbs) is very optimistic. The layout shown on the attached sheet would appear to have the following characteristics:

(a) Lighter and within Wibault's assumed weight
(b) Closely similar performance
(c) Utilises a compressor under development
(d) Easier to install
(e) Cheaper
(f) Easier to control

G.M. Lewis

Right and below: The historic sketch of the BE.48 and memo by a Bristol engineer which transformed the Gyroptère into the V/STOLs we know today./*Rolls-Royce*

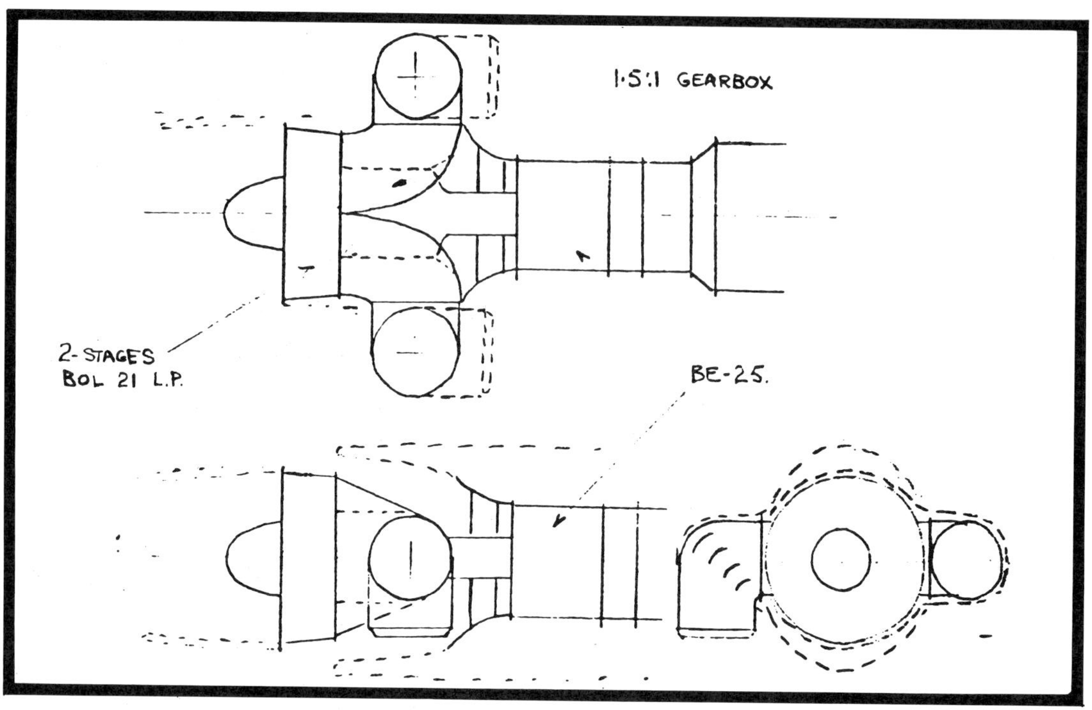

'vectored thrust with a jet.' Vectored thrust was not new, but this was the first time anyone had seen it on a jet aircraft – albeit one whose jets came from shaft-driven blowers. The consensus of opinion was that NATO and the Free World really needed a combat V/STOL, and the Frenchman's idea was sound; but he had perhaps not thought the actual design through sufficiently. It was a case for expert technical opinion. The people who came to mind first were Bristol Aero-Engines, whose Orpheus turbojet was standard engine for NBMR-1 (NATO Basic Military Requirement 1), a tactical fighter competition won by the Fiat G91. With Wibault's agreement, Chapman brought in Stanley Hooker.

Sir Stanley, a great Rolls-Royce engineer who had changed horses to become Technical Director at Bristol, had been keenly aware of jet V/STOL but could find no way to get into the act. The British government had plumped for the Rolls-Royce multiple lift-jet, or composite, scheme, which was in a monopoly position and protected by Derby patents. Hooker had occasionally had a few minutes to study V/STOL but had not put any of his project engineers on to this field. But he at once accepted Chapman's invitation to Paris in July 1956 and listened to the briefing. Wibault proposed a scheme which offered three important things: it offered a scheme for a single-engined flat-rising V/STOL; it was a true lift/propulsion engine with fully vectoring thrust; and the four nozzles could be ideally disposed about the cg (centre of gravity) of both the power unit and the aircraft. On the other hand, no engineer could warm to such a cumbersome and heavy arrangement with bevel gearboxes, shafting and rotating scrolls.

A week or two later a Bristol engineer, Gordon Lewis (today RR Director of Engineering at Bristol) had drawn a more elegant scheme which circumvented the clumsy features. He made the Orion drive through a reduction gearbox straight to a front fan formed from the first two stages of the big Olympus turbojet. This delivered air to left and right nozzles which could be vectored down through 90° to give lift. This project was designated Bristol BE.48, but though a great improvement it was still only a step along the road. Further study showed that, instead of an Orion, the drive could come from an Orpheus turbojet, a light and simple gas generator able to give about the same shaft-power for less weight and cost. Moreover, not only did this match ideally with the fan but the drive could come from a separate LP (low-pressure) turbine added behind the Orpheus and with its shaft fitting inside the existing tubular HP (high-pressure) shaft of the Orpheus. This enabled the reduction gearbox to be eliminated. Thus was born the BE.53.

This offered a vectored thrust of about 8,000lb, and was much more attractive than Wibault's arrangement. It was judged that a V/STOL military aircraft would have two of these engines, the total thrust then being great enough to lift a typical modern fighter/bomber. In late 1956 Hooker discussed the idea with the Ministry of Supply and with the parent Bristol Aeroplane Company board. Both were interested, but as the Ministry had no Service requirement there was little it could do – though Hooker formed the view that some kind of go-ahead within industry would be welcomed. After further refinement, at a low priority, and a typical British succession of official meetings that seemed to lack any objective, Hooker decided to talk to aircraft designers. He began with Hawker Aircraft.

This famous company at Kingston upon Thames had a global success in the Hunter fighter, and was in the process of spending £1million of its own money on a larger Mach 2 successor, the P.1121. For the first time the Chief of the Air Staff had not enthused over the next generation as proposed by the company's technical director, Sir Sydney Camm. With hindsight we can see that the P.1121 would have been a fine multi-role aircraft that in world markets would have given the F-4 Phantom a run for its money, as well as putting real muscle into the RAF. But the British official view had become polarised around the way that missiles could (it was thought) take the place of manned aircraft. Defence Minister Duncan Sandys was at that moment writing his famous – most people say infamous – White Paper that emerged on 4 April 1957. It said the RAF would be 'unlikely to require' any more manned fighters or bombers. There was one exception, a multi-role reconnaissance bomber that grew in size and weight until it was obvious the P.1121 could not meet the demands (it led to the TSR.2). In February 1957 Camm, and the Hawker Siddeley board big guns such as Sir Frank Spriggs and Sir Roy Dobson, were up against a stone wall. It seemed incredible that the prototype of a fine next-generation fighter/bomber should be actually taking shape at Kingston while the customer was refusing to show interest. And at this moment the BE.53 brochure landed on Camm's desk.

Camm is probably the most famous of all British aircraft designers. Though he was a great engineer who loved the elegance of simple design, and a great teacher who commanded respect and affection among his staff, he was a rather untypical aircraft person. Because of his intense care for the Hawker reputation and the lives of future pilots he tended to dislike and distrust new ideas. He wrote a brief memo, clipped it to the brochure and passed it to Ralph Hooper. Then he got on with the mainstream: trying to turn the P.1121 into the twin-engine, two seat P.1129 to win the only military-aircraft deal in prospect.

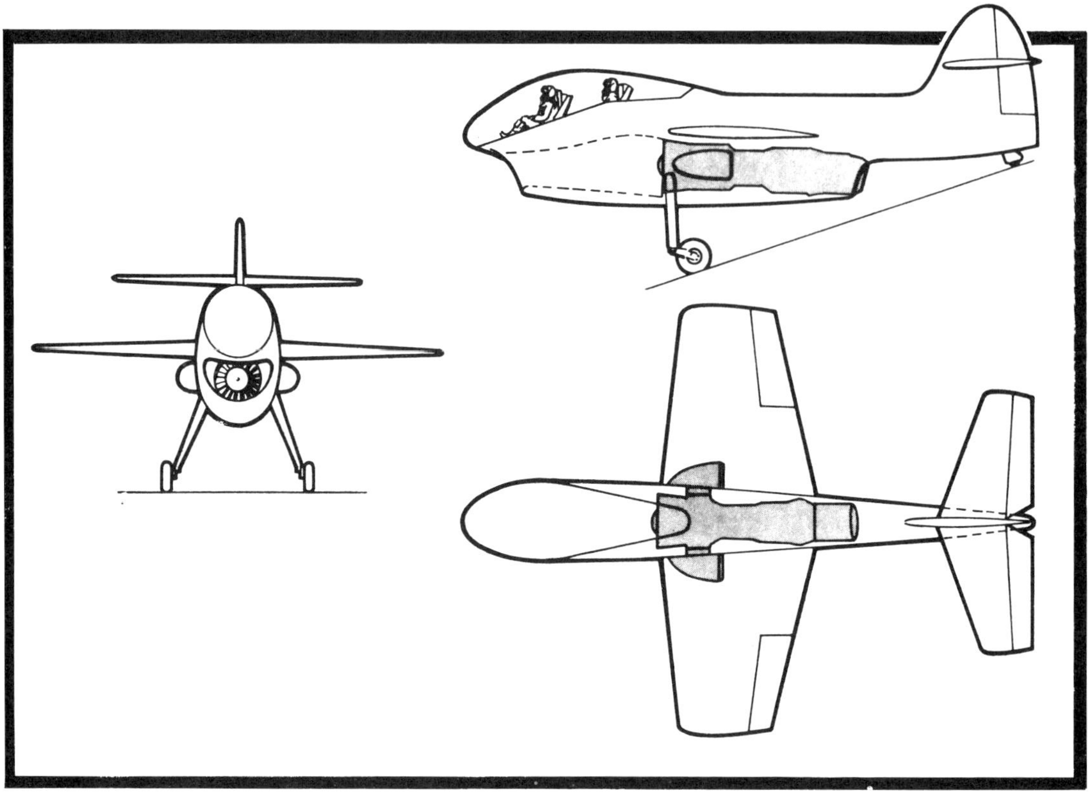

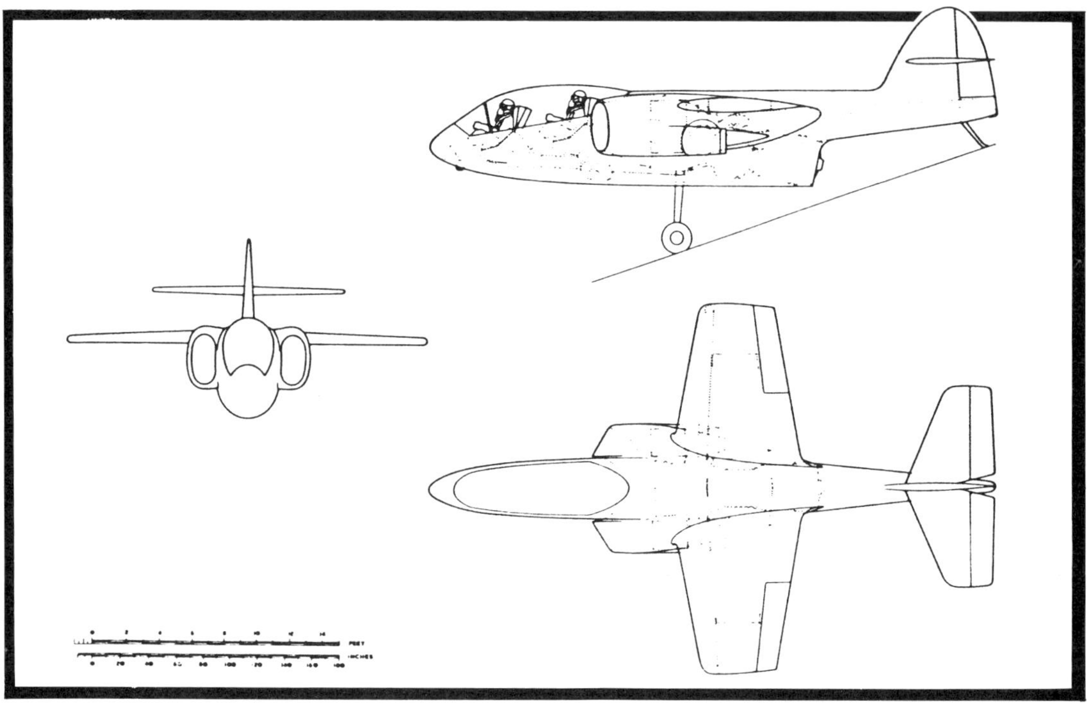

Hooper and his colleague and office-sharer John Fozard (former Project Engineer P.1121, and then chief ulcer-getter on the 1129) were not terribly impressed by the BE.53. The thrust at the rear had to be cancelled by rotating the two vectored nozzles through well over 100° to blast partly forwards, and this reduced the available lift in VTO. The nozzles themselves were clumsy bent elbows to which were attached long upstream fairings which were very unattractive in the VTO mode in which the aircraft had to accelerate to high forward speed with nozzles deflected. By March 1957 Hooper had drawn a three-view of a project designated P.1127 but this was clearly not going to carry much, nor fly far, nor reach high speeds. The whole thing might have been dropped, but the vital need for a long-term future project kept it alive; and, as the future of the 1121 and 1129 became bleaker, so did the 1127 gain momentum.

Left: The very first P.1127 three-view, prepared by Ralph Hooper at Kingston in March 1957./*BAe*

Below left: A month later a more attractive solution had been found, though it was still incapable of VTOL./*Rolls-Royce*

Below: By June 1957 pressure from Hawker Aircraft had led to the novel idea of 'four-poster' thrust and lift from two pairs of nozzles ganged together. This was the aircraft that resulted./*BAe*

Fozard hit on the idea of bifurcating the jetpipe, as had been done on an earlier Hawker fighter, the Sea Hawk, to discharge through a second pair of vectoring nozzles rotating in unison with the first. He also knew that nozzles can be smaller and lighter if they contain a cascade of multiple curved vanes to turn the flow, and drew a new engine with five-vane nozzles giving 'four-poster' lift. Timidly the idea was put to Bristol. As there was no response, the suggestion was put more loudly, together with the belief that it would be a good idea if the LP and HP spools rotated in opposite directions. This would reduce if not cancel out the engine's gyroscopic torque, which the Hawker engineers could see would be very powerful on a small hovering aircraft whose fuselage axis could pivot rapidly. This time there was a response: the engine designers said the bearings would not take the loads. But by this time Kingston and Bristol were constantly talking, and after about six months the engine team went along with not only the four-poster idea but also contra-rotation. A new fan was designed with mirror-image blading to rotate in the opposite direction. As a result, the resultant gyroscopic couple fell close to zero. Another advance, by the engine team, was to use a common inlet for the whole engine flow, so that the fan supercharged the core. Engine weight was reduced, and the plenum chamber downstream of the fan delivered compressed air to the front nozzles and the HP compressor, with minimum

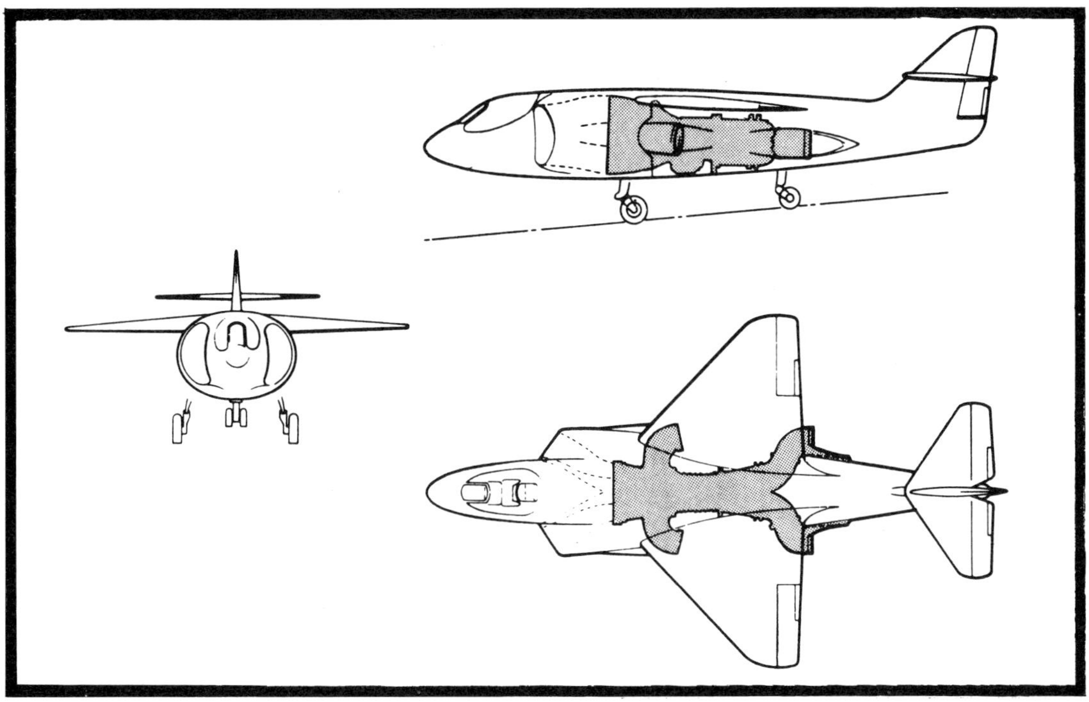

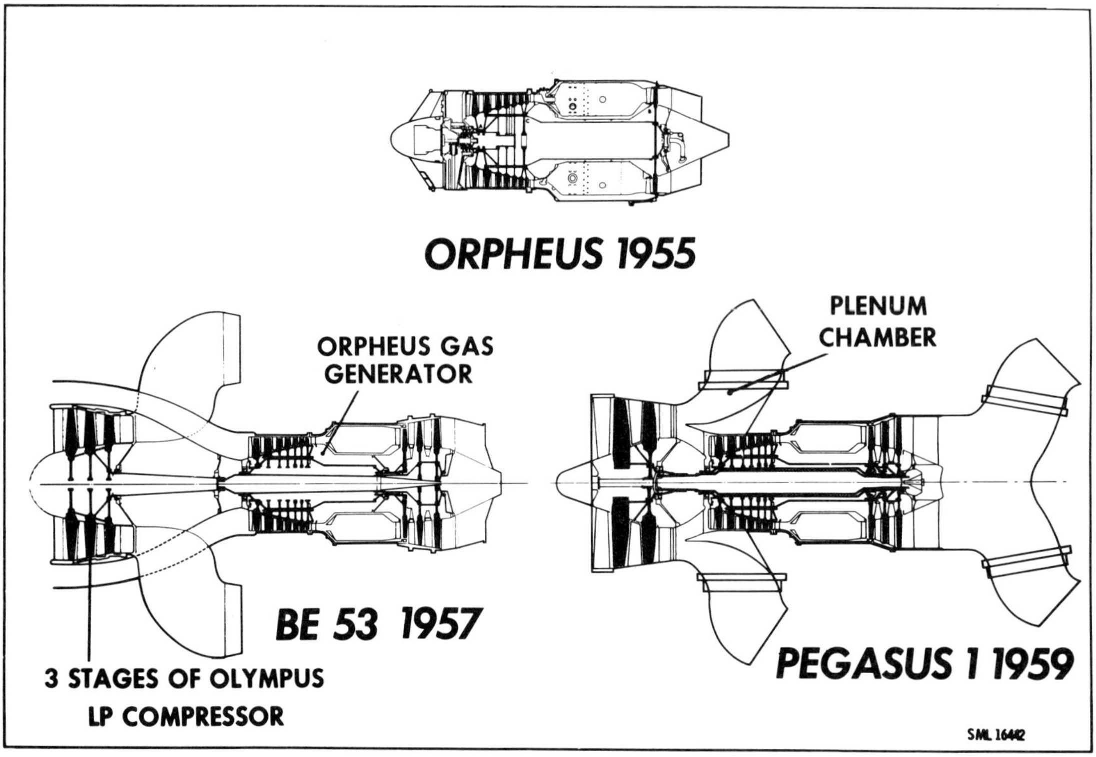

frontal area and installation problems. The engine was designed BE.53/2.

The ultimate form of the original aircraft studies was abandoned in June 1957 and replaced by a more attractive machine with four-poster jet lift from the BE.53/2 engine. This could achieve VTOL, and the first complete drawing of this family dates from August 1957. Engine thrust for VTOL had risen in this configuration to 9,000lb, but some juggling with bypass ratio (the ratio of flows through the front and rear nozzles) was needed to adjust the flows so that the jets from the front nozzles (which in today's Harrier are at about the temperature of boiling water) gave about the same thrust as the two hot-gas jets at the rear. The bypass ratio to do this was around 1.35:1. In early 1958 the Bristol board decided that, though the whole thing still looked fraught with problems for no evident market, they would go ahead with a BE.53 design if funding could be found for three-quarters of the cost. MWDP promptly agreed, Bristol paying the other 25 per cent. The initial programme comprised six engines, two for bench testing and four for flight. Though the estimated development bill escalated, as these things have a habit of doing, neither MWDP (on behalf of the US taxpayer) not the Bristol company wavered in their faith and

Above: The concept of vectored-thrust V/STOL links the engine and aircraft in a new way. These Bristol drawings show how the world's first purpose-designed jet lift/cruise engine evolved./*Rolls-Royce*

Above right: By early 1958 the P.1127 had reached its familiar form, though many changes were yet to follow. Hardly a single part is common to any of today's Harriers./*BAe*

Below: There was tight control on the P.1127 development budget, but it had to stretch to include a tunnel model to explore the overall effect of the puffing and blowing which was unprecedented in its variability./*BAe*

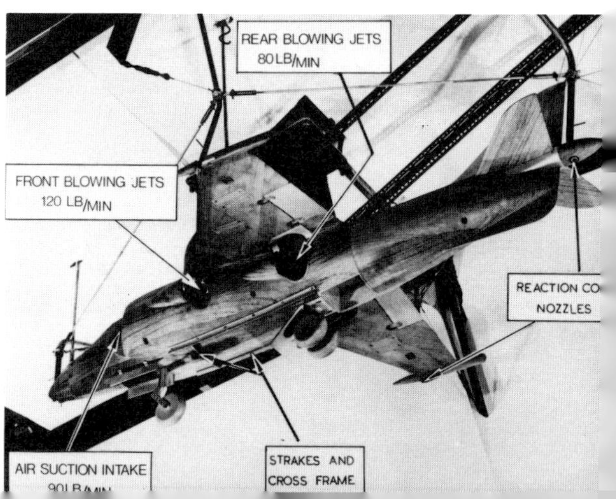

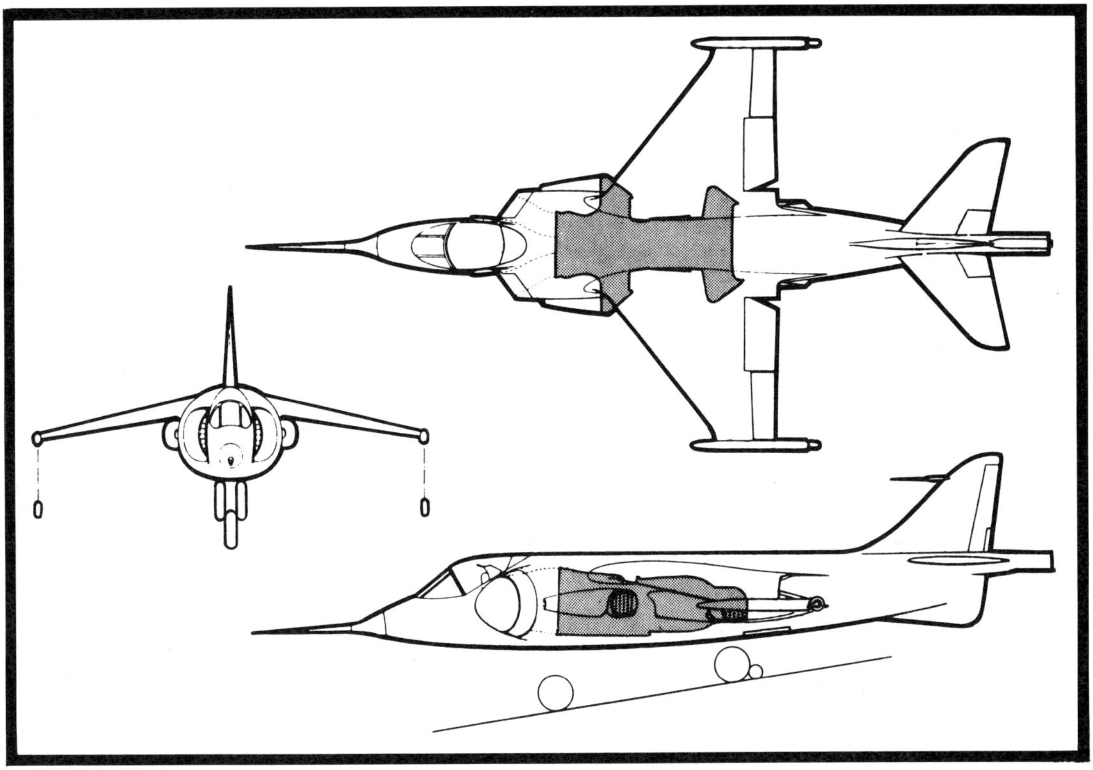

determination, and the first BE.53/2, by this time named Pegasus 1, ran at Patchway, Bristol, in September 1959.

Gradually Camm had allowed more and more of his engineers to work on the P.1127, though he still showed even less enthusiasm for the weird bird than he tended to show for any new project. For two years Hawker Siddeley's board allowed design study and then actual engineering design to continue at company expense. By 1958 a major change had spun off to alter the engine. A V/STOL needs jet reaction control valves (RCVs) at its extremities to impart forces to control it in hovering flight, when ordinary control surfaces have no effect (because there is little or no airflow over them). The obvious way to arrange reaction controls is to feed the RCVs with air bled from the engine. Hooper bled off fan air through aluminium pipes which seemed to be the best solution, but it was found that, to get the RCV thrust needed, the pipes had to be too large to fit inside the airframe! The only answer was to bleed air at much higher pressure and temperature from the HP delivery and take it through pipes of stainless steel. A continuous-bleed system was adopted, feeding RCVs blowing downwards (to add to the lift) at the wingtips and nose and tail, the two latter valves being able to swivel laterally to control the aircraft in yaw.

In March 1959, in the continuing absence of official interest, Hawker Siddeley took the courageous decision to commit funds to the manufacture of two prototype P.1127s, and drawings were released to the Kingston experimental shops in the same month. The design had crystalised as a necessarily small and simple machine, with the engine on the centre of gravity, the wing above the engine, bicycle landing gear with wingtip outriggers, and an airframe designed to the same limits as the Hunter of 620 knots EAS/Mach 1. In fact it was doubtful that it would be able to reach these limits in level flight, but it was still reasonable to regard the 1127 as a light ground-attack aircraft rather than a pure research machine. It was sad that neither the Ministry nor RAF were allowed, by their own choice, to show any interest in such an aircraft, but at Fontainebleau and in Paris the NATO staff were drafting NBMR-3, a new basic military requirement for an aircraft to replace the G91. V/STOL capability was by 1959 seen as a desirable, if not essential, attribute. Thanks to Britain's allies the funding – which soon exceeded $10million – kept the engine on schedule. Hawker, having already lost £1million on the P.1121, began to detect a faint thaw in ministerial corridors by 1960, as officials began to feel their careers might not be imperilled by daring to talk to Hawker about the P.1127.

To meet the demand for HP bleed air Bristol had changed the core from the Orpheus 3 to that of the dimensionally similar Orpheus 6, which in turn required a rematched two-stage HP turbine in an engine called Pegasus 2 (BE.53/3). The first 53/3 ran in February 1960, giving 11,000lb thrust. But then a new problem emerged: preliminary tunnel testing and various theoretical calculations suggested that the aircraft would be unstable. When accelerating ahead from VTO, in partially wingborne flight with the jets at an intermediate angle, the P.1127 appeared liable to run into uncontrollable divergence in pitch, and tumble nose-over-tail. There was a chance that a skilled pilot might be able to accelerate through the 'impossible' regime fast enough to avoid disaster, but this is no way to design aeroplanes. British government tunnels were not allowed to be involved, but it so happened that one of the great American aerodynamicists, NASA's John Stack, had become excited at the possibilities of both the P.1127 and its value as a research tool in his own tunnels. He authorised the construction by NASA of a one-sixth model of the P.1127, complete with jet nozzles fed from two internal fans driven by HP air acting on tip turbine blades. It was the nearest possible approach to a real 1127, and Marion McKinney put it in the great 30ft by 60ft tunnel at Langley and on 18 January 1960 began the first really large and detailed P.1127 aircraft test programme. Eventually the model was being flown by four pilots, seated in cubicles round the working section and each controlling one variable. By 4 February a complete forwards transition had been made from VTO into wingborne flight, with no trouble except when the air hose broke free and blasted the model with air at 300lb/sq in. NASA also built a smaller metal model tested in a transonic tunnel, and did STO and rolling landing tests out of doors on a giant whirling arm. They let Hawker chief test pilot A. W. (Bill) Bedford and colleague Hugh Merewether fly the Bell X-14 and a variable-stability helicopter, and play with a simulator programmed to fly like a P.1127.

Maybe all this positive assistance helped in shaming the British officials into taking notice. In June 1960 the Ministry of Supply at last decided the kingdom might not be endangered if it provided financial cover for the two P.1127s, and it not only repaid the Hawker board their costs but issued serial numbers XP831 and 836, and drafted a contract. It had to be made clear that the P.1127 was not actually a light ground-attack fighter, or any other kind of manned military aircraft, but a pure research machine; and the Experimental Requirement ER.204D was duly issued. Then the officials were thrown into a panic by

Above: XP831 at Richmond Road before it was taken to Dunsfold; the photograph shows the first trial fit of a BE.53 engine./*BAe*

Above right: XP831 hovering in October 1960, unpainted except for black/white camera targets and with tufted rear fuselage./*BAe*

Centre right: By the time it reached RAE Bedford the first aircraft had a presentable appearance; it is pictured with the RAT extended. /*BAe*

Bottom right: Ground-effect model sucking at two inlets and blowing at four jets; note the date./*BAe*

the fact that the Pegasus engine had not been designed to British official requirements, and was not covered by the necessary documentation. By August the necessary paperwork had been created, and the Pegasus 2 cleared at 11,000lb for 15 hours of flight in the VTO mode or 20 hours in conventional flight.

XP831 was completed with temporary bellmouth air inlets to ensure good airflow. Despite this, the margin between installed thrust and gross weight was very small, and even the radio was removed and replaced by a ground intercom link. It was wheeled out to a metal grid flush with the surface of the company airfield at Dunsfold, Surrey, and tethered by the outrigger and nose gears to weights locked under the grid. After engine running and shakedown tests, Bedford – with a broken leg in plaster – lifted the wheels off the ground on 21 October 1960.

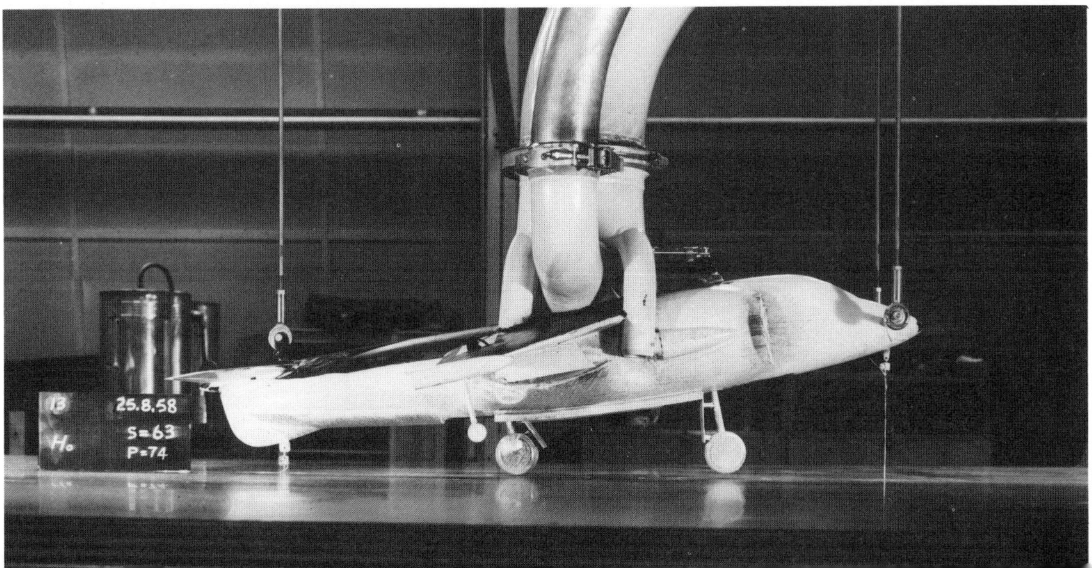
13
25.8.58
Ho
S=63
P=74

2 The Kestrel

The initial flying of the first P.1127 was shared by Bedford and Merewether, who took over as chief test pilot in 1967. It was at once clear that, though the problems were not quite as hair-raising as on the NASA simulator, hovering control was not all it might be. The swivelling nose and tail RCVs were quite unable, even with a whole bootful of rudder pedal, to counter the inlet momentum drag and stop the aircraft pirouetting round tail-on to the breeze. The fact that each time one of the tethers was pulled out to full stretch it injected a sudden snatch load at one of the attachments made hovering a full-time job. Merewether said it was 'rather like trying to master a bicycle in childhood by riding down a narrow corridor'. Not least of the problems was that at rest the aircraft tipped sideways on to one outrigger, and as the throttle was opened there was inadequate roll-control to bring the wings level so that, instead of lifting upwards, XP831 slid sideways, scrubbing the tyres across the grid.

Standing further back the problems were even greater. The 1957 Defence White Paper continued to cast a long shadow. It had made the whole programme very difficult to start, eliminated the possibility of normal British funding except on a basis of pure research, and severed normal links between the manufacturer and a military customer such as the RAF or Royal Navy. Stemming from this, Camm had been constrained to kick off with the smallest aircraft possible, without any real military capability. This compounded the RAF's lack of interest, which was made total by the pervading belief that, if it did have any future manned aircraft, such aircraft had to exceed Mach 2, a belief which for the ten years 1958-68 also excluded the excellent Buccaneer from being acceptable to the RAF. Had the RAF not so misled the gullible Defence Minister back in 1957 and kept an open mind on procurement there is no doubt the P.1127 could have been a different beast from the start and had two engines, or a bigger engine, and been a highly potent weapon platform. The flight development would still have been a major task, but it would have started with a different attitude and a different objective linked to early operational use.

As it was, the first P.1127 was not so much an impressive achievement as a demonstration of future potential, and the tragedy was that for silly political reasons the important decision-takers were forbidden to see the potential or show enthusiasm. The creation by Camm and Hooker out of Wibault was small, noisy and quite new in appearance, but in most respects it was not a 'first'. It made little use of any previous technology, but had in fact been preceded by numerous V/STOL aircraft as shown in the list on this page.

Above right: XP972 introduced a new wing and revised deflector fairings downstream of the hot rear nozzles./*BAe*

Right: By 1961 XP831 had most of the missing parts restored, insignia applied and the tail parachute added. Here the RAT (ram-air turbine) can be seen extended ahead of the fin./*BAe*

Some VTOL 'Firsts'

aircraft	*first flight*	*accomplishment*
Bachem Ba349 Natter	1944	VTO fighter
XFV-1/XFY-1	1953	VTO fighter with hovering capability
Deflected-jet Meteor	1954	Vectored-thrust main engines (not VTOL)
Bell VTO experimental	1954	Jet flat-riser VTOL with pivoting engines and air-bleed stabilisation system
R-R Flying Bedstead	1954	Stablisation airbleed from main engines
Ryan X-13 Vertijet	1957	High-speed (500 mph) single-jet VTOL, achieved transition to and from wing-supported flight
Bell X-14	1957	Jet flat-riser VTOL with vectored thrust; also achieved transition

XP972

XP831

XP980

XP831
Hawker P.1127

It was in the overall conception that the P.1127 offered new capability. It was not an impractical tail-sitter but a flat-riser. It was not a low-speed research aircraft but potentially as fast as such fighters as the Sabre and Hunter. It was inherently simple, with a single engine. Where it did break new ground was that the pilot had a new flight control. Back at Kingston in 1958 there had been great arguments about whether the P.1127 should have a helicopter-type collective lever, with the throttle as a twist-grip on the end. At last it was decided to use a conventional throttle working in a ratchet box containing a hydraulic dashpot and spring. To go from lift to thrust the hydraulic valve was shut, and the spring slowly rotated the nozzles from the downwards-pointing VTO mode to the rearwards-pointing forward-flight mode in 20-30 seconds without the pilot taking his hand off the throttle. To go from thrust to lift the pilot moved the throttle to the rear, and with the valve open the nozzles rotated immediately under the influence of the spring on the control system. During 1961 the dashpot was eliminated, then the ratchet, and finally the pilot ended up with a much better box carrying two levers, a normal throttle and a precise and immediate nozzle lever.

Bedford had gone along with Camm's belief that flying should start in the hovering mode, and for this reason 831 had been completed with the large bell-mouth inlets. Each time the bird rose above its grid much was learned, and modifications followed at a rapid pace. On 19 November 1960 the hated tethers came off – Camm said they had been put there at the insistence of the Ministry – and Bedford found it was 'like freeing a bird from a cage'. Free hovers became daily surer and more accurate until the time came to attack the problem from the other end: in conventional flight. XP831 went back into the shops for a complete rebuild of the RCV system and many other parts, emerging with an intermittent-bleed system and new yaw RCVs at the tail, driven by the rudder to squirt left/right in place of the swivelling pitch RCVs. But fast taxi tests showed terrible problems with freedom in roll, caused by the main gear hanging lower than the outriggers, poor nosewheel steering and severe shimmy (sideways oscillation) by the outriggers. Wavy lines left by molten rubber scarred Dunsfold, but various fixes had eased things when the aircraft went to the RAE (Royal Aircraft Establishment) at Bedford in March 1961. Still with the bell-mouth inlets, Bill Bedford made the first takeoff on 13 March, lifting off at at least 150 knots with flaps up to avoid powerful nose-down pitch, and incidentally far out-accelerating the chase Hunter.

In July 1961 the second aircraft, XP836, took its place in the flying schedule. Everything worked in 836, all the fairings were on, and the inlets were sharp-lipped for high-speed flight. This aircraft made conventional takeoffs and progressively brought the speed down close to the stall at around 90 knots; 831 made VTOs and progressively accelerated ahead to speeds closer and closer to 90 knots, the pilots 'cracking' (vectoring) the nozzles with more and more confidence. Finally in early September 1961 the two sets of trials met, and on the 12 September Bedford and Merewether each made complete accelerating and decelerating transitions. The Ministry sent an angry letter because it had been done without their permission; Bedford apologised and explained that he had decided it was better to go on and fly on the wings than try and stop in the remaining length of the airfield!

This was the first time a transonic aircraft had accomplished transition to and from V/STOL flight. Henceforth the P.1127 could fly at any speed from about 20 knots backwards to speeds close to that of sound. In fact, though it was not a specific design objective, the 1127 exceeded the speed of sound in December 1961 and a few days later reached Mach 1.2 in a dive.

While this was in progress much was going on elsewhere. In late 1960 the Ministry of Supply had funded four additional P.1127s, and for the first time openly called them not 'research aircraft' but 'development aircraft', the nuance suggesting that there might be some kind of operational military aircraft at the end of the road. In France the NATO staffs had decided the future did indeed lie with V/STOL, and in March 1961 issued two Basic Military Requirements that could have transformed the NATO air forces. NBMR-3 called for a V/STOL close-support strike fighter, and NBMR-4 for a V/STOL transport. What happened to this bold objective is outlined in the next chapter.

From 1961 the NBMR-3 programme dominated most of the air staffs and planemakers in the NATO nations, including Camm and Hooker. The P.1127 became mentally downgraded to the status of the small research aircraft that would underpin the much more advanced machine with supersonic performance to meet the NBMR-3 requirement. In 1961 nobody expected a military aircraft to emerge directly from the P.1127 and Pegasus except perhaps a training or indoctrination machine. This view was strongly

Above left: XP980 was not a Kestrel but the fifth P.1127, though it had various Kestrel features such as tailplane anhedral and ventral strakes. It is seen with black rubber-bag inflatable intakes./*BAe*

Left: Inflatable engine inlets were fitted to the first P.1127 by the time it went to sea for the first time, aboard *Ark Royal*. The wing has been modified and ventral strakes fitted, but the tailplane is horizontal. /*BAe*

Above: The short-lived second prototype, with its glass-fibre nozzles at 60°./*BAe*

Far right: The first production Valiant was used as a flying testbed for the Pegasus 2 and 3 which was installed in a pod that made no attempt to duplicate the P.1127./*Rolls-Royce*

broadcast by the RAF, which did not regard the single-Pegasus aircraft as worthy of consideration – though there was interest in the NBMR-3 because this was supersonic, impressive, and not subject to the taboo of the British Defence White Paper.

This is a convenient place at which to record the many changes in the airframe and engine companies. In 1963 Hawker Aircraft Ltd became the Hawker Blackburn Division of Hawker Siddeley Aviation (HSA). In 1965 HSA was reorganised into a single company, remaining such until in 1977 it became the Kingston-Brough Division of British Aerospace, which in turn is now BAe (PC) Ltd. As for the engine supplier, Bristol Aero-Engines merged with Armstrong Sideley Motors in April 1959 to form Bristol Siddeley Engines Ltd (BSEL), the BE.53 subsequently being designated BS.53. Later BSEL swallowed de Havilland Engines and Blackburn Engines and, unfortunately, was in turn absorbed in 1966 into a gigantically expanded Rolls-Royce Ltd. It retained some identity as Bristol Engine Division (BED) until in 1976 it became merely a major part of the Rolls-Royce Aero Division. Fortunately the people who actually did the work survived these traumatic changes without too many unnecessary extra problems.

One of BSEL's early changes to the Pegasus was to change the material of the front nozzles from glass-fibre reinforced plastics (GRP) to steel. This was because, on 14 December 1961, while Bill Bedford was flying the second P.1127 over Somerset, the left front nozzle came off. RNAS (Royal Naval Air Station) Yeovilton was handy and Bedford tried to make an immediate landing. Merewether, flying chase, did not see the nozzle missing or he would have said 'No flaps,' because of the asymmetry. With flaps lowered and speed reduced the P.1127 entered a roll which could not be corrected, and ejection was the only answer.

There were further incidents in which the engine played a part. On 30 October 1962 Merewether was engaged in tight turns in XP972, the third aircraft, when the compressor blades rubbed on the casing and started the first-ever titanium fire. Merewether did not eject but pointed the aircraft at RAF Tangmere, just as Neville Duke, a former Hawker chief test pilot, had done with a Hunter a decade earlier. The gear was extended by emergency air at the last moment and failed to lock, but the aircraft was to fly again. Far more public was the maddening failure of the nozzle-motor control system as Bedford was hovering in the original prototype in front of about 110,000 people at the 1963 Paris Air Show. All four nozzles rotated to the rear, quite slowly but still too fast to give the aircraft significant forward speed so that the wing could lift. The P.1127 slumped to the ground hard enough to be said to have crashed. The cause was a speck of grit in the nozzle air-motor servo. Later this aircraft too was repaired, as outlined in the Appendices at the back of this book.

From the start the United States aircraft industry and Department of Defense watched the P.1127 closely, because, though it could be good for the West, at the same time it presented commercial competition in a field where the British engine companies held powerful patents. On 14 January 1961 a joint announcement by the newly created British Ministry

of Aviation and Federal German government proclaimed imminent negotiations for 'joint development of a VTOL lightweight strike fighter on the basis of the P.1127.' The British Minister, Peter Thorneycroft, then at once moved on from Bonn to Rome. This triggered reactions in Washington, where for four years British military aircraft development had on Britain's own insistence been virtually discounted. The little Hawker project appeared to be a good thing to be involved with – though to what extent the motivation was one of avoiding difficult competition is hard to judge. The American response, pushed especially strongly by the Army, eventually materialised as the suggestion that Britain, the US and Federal Germany should jointly fund a Tripartite Evaluation Squadron (TES) to be 'equipped with aircraft of P.1127 or similar type' and with personnel drawn from the three national armed forces.

Thus in early 1962 things appeared at last to be moving, and in several directions. In Britain the paper study of an 'ultimate P.1127,' drafted in 1959 as Operational Requirement 345, merely to see how such an aircraft might perform and what it could do for the RAF, was cancelled, without its existence ever having become known to the public. This was because the RAF continued to be polarised around Mach 2, and henceforth put all its talents and operational planning into the P.1154, as described in the next chapter. Germany, the United States and Italy, however, viewed the P.1127 with intense interest. Northrop, sensing possible adoption by either the USAF or US Army (and the latter saw in the British project a way of evading the restrictions on its fixed-wing equipment), announced in January 1962 it was collaborating with Hawker on V/STOL strike fighters and would build the P.1127 in the event of an American order.

From before the start of hovering tests in 1960 it had been evident that 12,000lb was inadequate thrust for a useful single-engined V/STOL, and Bristol Siddeley accordingly developed the Pegasus 3, which ran on the bench in April 1961 and flew in April 1962 with an initial cleared life of 30 hours. Its chief modification was a new HP spool, with an eighth stage added at the rear of the compressor and a second stage added to the turbine. This gave a rating of 13,500lb, shortly uprated to 14,000lb. Much of the basic development of the Pegasus was undertaken on testbeds at Patchway on which the engine or nozzles were inverted, to blast either to the rear or upwards, thus avoiding ground erosion and disturbance around the bed. Other than in the P.1127s all early flight development was carried out with the first production Valiant WP199, which was rebuilt to carry a Pegasus

XS688

Left: In 1962 the first and third aircraft were flying with black inlet lips of inflatable rubber, to reconcile the conflicting demands of hovering and high-speed flight. Seen here on XP972, they were not a success. */BAe*

Right: The P.1127 suffered from poor static stability due to the destabilising effect of the jets passing under the tailplane and severe pitch-up at transonic speed. Vortex generators were added, next came a 'poor-man's streamwise tip' and in the Kestrel a new swept wing.*/BAe*

Below left: The first Kestrel had the 44.2 sq ft tailplane and lacked various other features that became standard. The insignia was assembled from that of the three participating nations.*/Rolls-Royce*

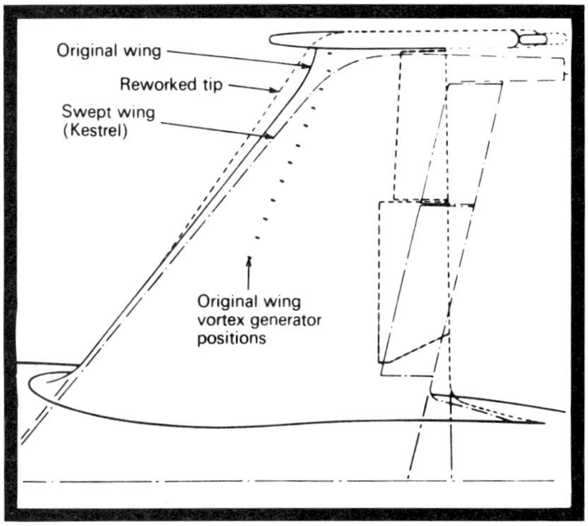

in the modified weapon bay, so that the four nozzles were correctly disposed around the cg.

With the Pegasus 3 the whole V/STOL flight envelope of the P.1127 could be explored, and it was this engine that accomplished the bulk of the aircraft-development and research flying prior to 1965. It was fitted to the last three P.1127s – which were much needed, because by 1963 the first three were, even if only temporarily, *hors de combat* – and these also incorporated various aerodynamic, structure and systems changes that the early flying had shown to be needed. In 1962 prolonged efforts were made to perfect an inflatable rubber lip to the inlets, rather like a pneumatic airframe de-icer, which could lie flush in cruising flight but be inflated in the jetborne mode. When deflated they always rippled and became torn off, and this idea was ultimately abandoned. The fourth aircraft had a revised wing with slightly kinked leading edges giving reduced taper outboard. Changes were made to the outrigger stabilizing gears, RCV fairings, engine inlets, larger anhedral tailplane and Küchemann low-drag wingtips.

On 21 May 1962 Ministry of Aviation contract FGA.236 ordered nine (reduced from 18 to save money) further-developed aircraft named Kestrel, to equip the TES. These were to fly with at least some military load, and to operate under all weather conditions practicable for a basic VFR aircraft. Bristol Siddeley accordingly had to pull out still more thrust, and in June 1962 the first Pegasus 5 ran on the bench to mark the beginning of the final and most important phase of thrust-development. The fan was no longer based on the Olympus but as a completely new unit with three stages, without any inlet guide vanes, at the time a bold innovation. Variable inlet guide vanes were added upstream of the HP compressor, whose blading was all-titanium, the combustion chamber was a new fully annular type with vaporising burners, and the first-stage HP turbine was given aircooled blades. The Pegasus 5 was designed for 18,000lb thrust but for the TES it was derated to 15,500lb to save time and money. The engine first flew in February 1964.

Equally major changes took place in the design of the Kestrel. The most important was a new wing, with a swept planform and thicker root which altered the 'sit' of the aircraft and gave a humped top line to the fuselage. The fuselage was lengthened by splicing in extra bays above the front nozzles and below the rear nozzles which had the effect of shifting the wing rearwards. The engine was given a sharper jetpipe bifurcation to move the rear (hot) nozzles forwards, and the overall result was a better relationship between aircraft cg, wing cp (centre of pressure, through which the overall lift acts) and the engine nozzles. Ventral strakes, retroactively fitted to the P.1127s, improved flow and increased pressure under the belly in low-altitude hovering. The landing gear was fitted with a new door stressed for unrestricted operation as an airbrake, and like the 1127 with low-pressure tyres for flying from unpaved surfaces. Under the wings could be bolted two stores pylons, and the nose did not carry a long instrumentation boom but housed a forward-oblique camera. For reasons of 'cost and timescale' the MoA unfortunately omitted autostabilization from the Kestrel flight-control system, despite the fact that P.1127 flying had demonstrated its value in reducing pilot work-load.

The first Kestrel F(GA).1 (Fighter, Ground Attack) flew on 7 March 1964, right on the heels of the last P.1127 – in fact, the latter aircraft was virtually a Kestrel itself, and all the surviving P.1127s

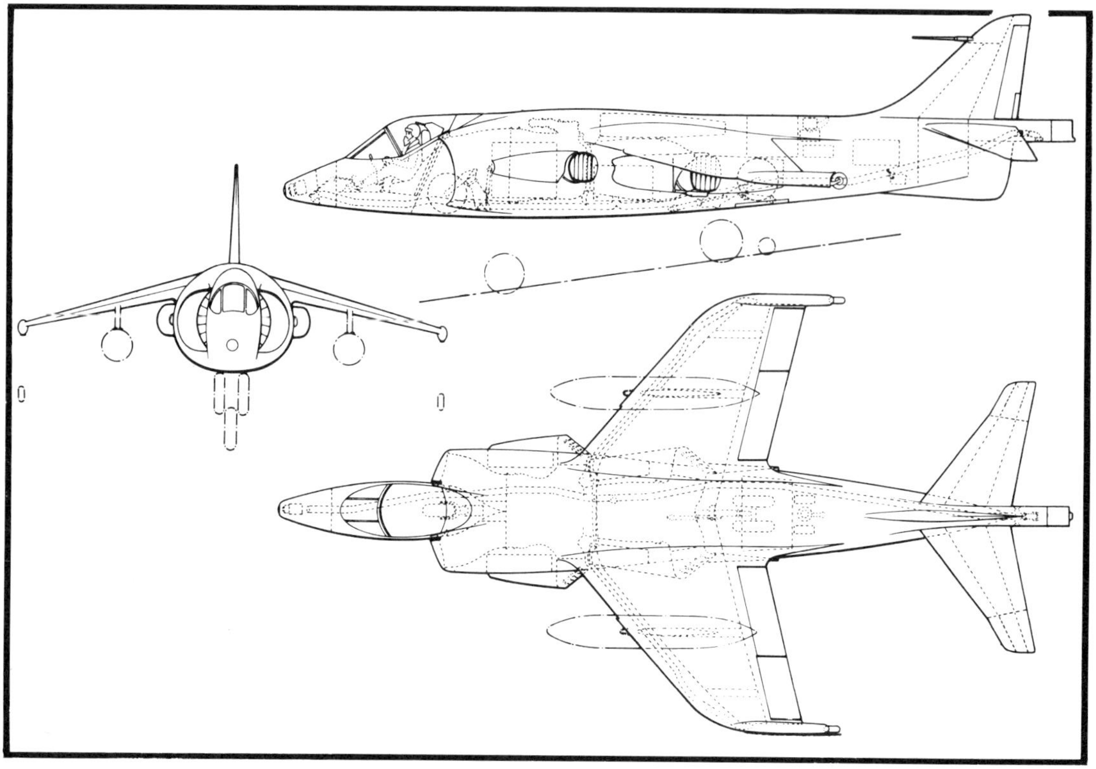

had by this time been considerably modified compared with the original standard. In December 1964 the Kestrel was given full CA Release (clearance for Service operations, signed by the MoA Controller, Aircraft). This clearance was unrestricted, and it was the first ever issued for any kind of jet-lift or V/STOL aircraft other than those having rotating wings.

The TES received the last P.1127 as well as the nine Kestrels, and formed at Dunsfold, on 15 October 1964, under the CO, Wing Commander D.McL. Scrimgeour RAF. After training, the squadron moved to RAF West Raynham, Norfolk, and began operational evaluation in April 1965. Pilots and ground personnel of the RAF, USAF, US Navy and

Above: The final form of Kestrel had the same tailplane as the single-seat Harriers of today; but almost everything else differs./*BAe*

Right: While an uninformed observer might have thought the TES did nothing but 'play at V/STOL' in fact it was the first unit ever to provide answers to countless piloting, logistic and operational unknowns./*BAe*

Below: The Tripartite Evaluation Squadron (TES) flight line at RAF West Raynham, Norfolk, in early 1965, with five Kestrels in the lineup.

US Army (but no Marines) and Luftwaffe accomplished most of the things they could do with aircraft not actually equipped to fire guns or deliver weapons, except occasional practice bombs, though the syllabus was primitive and did not include many important missions or techniques that could have been at least simulated if not actually carried out. The basic task assigned to the TES was to assess the practical merits and difficulties of jet V/STOL and see what it felt like, what it could do, and what problems appeared to be soluble or otherwise. Considerable emphasis was placed on off-airfield operations, studying dispersal, camouflage, logistic supply and how to live under canvas (something Western air forces had forgotten).

About 600 hours were flown in 938 missions in the formal TES programme, completed in November 1965. Further flying was carried out between then and April 1966 when six Kestrels were shipped to the United States. They were bought at the very low 'used price' written into the original tripartite agreement, the Federal German Defence Ministry having declined to purchase its three alotted aircraft which were transferred to the United States. One Kestrel had been written off, and the remaining pair were transferred from the RAF back to MoA charge, one going to Hawker Siddeley at Brough for re-engining with the Pegasus 6 and the other conducting various trials at the BLEU (Blind Landing Experimental Unit) at Bedford, in company with an SC.1 jet V/STOL which used the Rolls-Royce scheme of a battery of separate lift jets. Preliminary research was then undertaken into the possibility of a jet-lift automatic-landing system.

In the United States the six Kestrels were designated Hawker Siddeley XV-6A and used, or misused, as pure research aircraft and hacks. Between March and July 1966 a considerable amount of XV-6A flying was accomplished, a fraction of it properly directed and very useful. A particular advance was made in operations from ships, as related in the chapter on the Sea Harrier, and in vectoring the engine nozzles in flight manoeuvres. Interesting fundamental research was accomplished by NASA, but the US military view of the XV-6A was coloured by the fact that it was foreign – and also a basic and limited aircraft rather than a fully fledged weapon system. Perhaps the importance of V/STOL is somewhat lost at bases with the biggest runways and some of the highest air temperatures in the world. Certainly the USAF strongly adhered to the view that V/STOL was not considered worth while, and in 1966 still expected the F-111 to sell all over the world as the next-generation all-can-do military aircraft. The arguments formulated at that time by the USAF did much to hold back V/STOL combat aircraft, and even today make it difficult for them to be judged objectively by many air forces.

3 Supersonic V/STOL

By 1959 NATO's air staffs had begun to realise that any future war in central Europe would almost certainly be signalled by the wiping off the map, by nuclear missiles, of 99 per cent of NATO's air power. This had injected urgency into the repeated revisions to NATO's draft specification for a future light multi-role tactical aircraft to succeed the Fiat G91. Jet V/STOL capability was written in, and while for a further year Mach 0.92 was deemed fast enough, by 1960 supersonic speed (if possible Mach 2) was being called for at medium and high altitudes.

Planemakers throughout the NATO alliance began to generate paper designs at a rate never seen since World War 2. They got together in groups, or avoided each other as enemies, while Bristol Siddeley and Rolls-Royce ran out of bright performance engineers able to talk to all the would-be customers. One of the design teams that got on by itself was that at Kingston. Camm had a sixth sense that warned him of future changes in staff thinking, and back in 1959 had talked to Hooker about vectored-thrust for supersonic flight. The engine man said that the best place for boosting the engine was not downstream of the turbine but in the fan airflow, which was pure air with 21 per cent oxygen still available. Instead of afterburning (reheat), Hooker recommended burning extra fuel between the fan and the cold front nozzles. This was named plenum-chamber burning (PCB).

By May 1960 Kingston had a firm proposal from Hooker for a PCB Pegasus 5 with a peak PCB temperature of 927°C, giving thrust raised from 15,500lb to 20,500lb. At the same time Hooker began an in-house study of a later and even more powerful engine, the BS.100, which incorporated discs and blades from the Olympus 22R, then in full development for TSR.2. Both the proposed engines were intended for V/STOL aircraft with supersonic capability. Both incorporated PCB, which is based on ramjet technology but involves high-intensity combustion around a curved path. The BS.100, intended for the post-1965 era, was an especially compact unit. Unlike the Pegasus its four nozzle axes were inclined downwards instead of sideways, reducing the angle through which the gas flow had to be turned and thus eliminating much of the pressure loss in the ducts and nozzles. The rear nozzles were well inboard, lying in the lee of the PCB front nozzles to reduce frontal area and drag. The front nozzles, in the aft (forwards flight) position, discharged past variable ramps which adjusted the nozzle area and minimized base drag.

Camm and Hooker preferred this all-new engine, but for reasons of timing had to stick to the PCB Pegasus. Working exactly to the latest draft NATO specification, Hooper laid out the Hawker P.1150, which apart from the stillborn Bell D-188A (XF-109) was the first supersonic V/STOL design in history. It was essentially a P.1127 type aircraft with much greater length, more fuel, a wing of reduced thickness/chord ratio with sweepback and streamwise Küchmann tips, a broader fuselage with extended sharp-lipped engine inlets, and two pylons under each wing. It was a totally different proposition from the P.1127 or Kestrel, but like most military customers the NATO staffs kept adding fresh requirements and making the numbers more severe. In March 1961 the NATO Basic Military Requirement 3 (NBMR-3) document was at last issued, providing exact guidelines for the contractor studies. It called for Mach 0.92 all round a lo-lo-lo (tree-top height) mission, with at least Mach 1.5 at medium height in the clean condition or armed with AAMs. A height of 50 feet was to be reached 500 feet from brakes-release with a weapon load of 2,000lb, with which the standard (lo-lo-lo) mission radius was to be not less than 250 nautical miles.

The radius with 2,000lb weapon load was just beyond the capability of the P.1150. Bristol Siddeley was by this time developing a better basic Pegasus, the Mk 6, with an all-titanium fan permitting higher rpm, water injection, aircooling to both sides of the HP turbine, two-vane exhaust nozzles, an improved combustion chamber, added fuel-system controls to limit temperatures and pressures, and a life recorder for monitoring creep. Rated at 19,000lb, this was a major jump in power, and with PCB promised to give

Right: Markedly larger than a Pegasus, the BS.100 also differed in having nozzles canted downwards instead of being on the lateral equator. This impressive engine first ran on 30 October 1964. */Rolls-Royce*

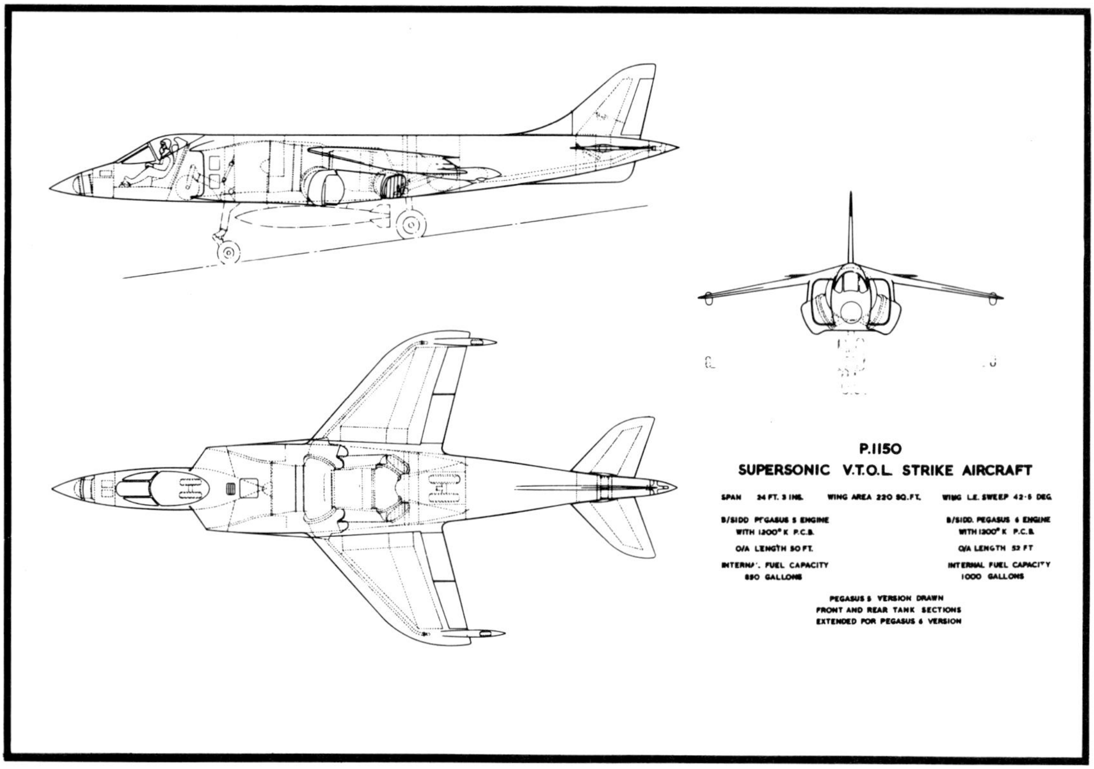

about 25,000lb. Hooper drew a stretched P.1150 using a PCB Pegasus 6 with greater fuel capacity as shown in the notes on the three-view drawing. Even this did not fully meet the requirement, and the P.1152 was studied with BS.59 lift fans in front of and behind the main engine. This work was carried out in partnership with Focke-Wulf, which was independently looking at the FW1262 with a lift/thrust BS.94 and two RB.162 lift jets (later other engines were substituted). Project piled upon project, and even after the contractual AC/169 document was sent to all bidders in August 1961, stipulating a deadline of 31 December of that year, more than 40 proposals were being worked on by 23 companies.

Of all these the surest and most refined proposal was one of the last to crystallise, the Hawker P.1154. This was a further stretch of the P.1150 designed around the new BS.100 engine, at first derated to just under 30,000lb thrust. Even at this modest rating, less than that for such rival designs as the Br.1115 and Fokker/Republic D.24 Allianz, the P.1154 easily exceeded all AC/169 requirements and appeared an outstanding basis on which to develop a warplane for the later 1960s. Hawker's comprehensive three-volume submission was made in January 1962.

From the start of the P.1127 programme Rolls-Royce had deemed it almost an affront that any other engine builder should try to offer competition, and for the first time set its face squarely against the British aircraft industry in promoting foreign designs using Derby engines. In this case the favoured project was the Dassault Mirage IIIV from France, and Rolls even managed to win-over a fair proportion of the British Air Staff which openly favoured the IIIV, whose candidature was backed by Sud-Aviation in France, Boeing in the USA and by the new consortium BAC as a potential licence-builder for RAF orders. A deeper problem was that the whole NBMR-3 bandwagon was just empty words. NATO had no funds, and could do no more than say which design the assessors considered to have won. In April 1962 the NATO Standing Group announced that on technical grounds the winner was the P.1154. At the same time, because there was bound to be an almighty outcry from France, NATO weakly said the Mirage IIIV was 'of equal merit'. The house of cards collapsed, most nations – notably including the United States – adopting the same posture as that adopted by world airlines when the Comet I brought jet speed and comfort in 1952: they trotted out every reason they could think of for adopting the role of passive observer.

This was one of the crucial periods in the V/STOL story. Though the United States continued to pour more than $1million every week into pure V/STOL research manifestly remote from any kind of warplane, the nation set its face steadfastly against the proven and immediate possibilities. In planning the TFX (which became the swing-wing F-111) and in many Congressional hearings the argument was repeated, parrot-fashion, that V/STOL meant oversized engines, poor range/payload and many other drawbacks. Air forces around the world continued to stick 100 per cent to CTOL (conventional takeoff and landing) aircraft unable to operate except from bases of known location. This attitude endures in the USAF to this day, just as if the hundreds of airfield-targeted Russian missiles did not exist!

Britain, however, did not suffer from the 'not invented here' mentality. The 1957 White Paper was five years in the background, and the fresh faces in the Whitehall corridors, and the new Air Staff, no longer felt their careers were in danger if they discussed the need for new fighter and attack aircraft. For two years the objective had seemed to be to concoct design proposals for a giant NATO competition. Now, as 1962 dawned, it was recognised that nothing would happen unless individual nations worked out some national requirements and put in some national funding. By March the Ministry of Defence had accepted the view that the P.1154 could probably replace the Hunter in the RAF and the Sea Vixen in the Royal Navy, and both Services were told to draft ORs (Operational Requirements) pretty smartly. The Minister, Harold Watkinson, was all for a collaborative programme, but Air Minister Amery wisely saw that round-table conferences could go on for ever, and put his weight behind a British go-ahead.

While Camm's team pushed ahead with refinements, studies and the start of engineering design, the two Services swiftly wrote separate ORs, OR.356 for the RAF and AW.406 for the Navy. Predictably they were like chalk and cheese: the Navy wanted a high-altitude air combat fighter with a crew of two, while the RAF wanted a low-level single-seater to hit surface targets. The Navy aircraft had to be carrier-compatible, but it was tragic that Navy demands – some later shown by experience with the Sea Harrier to have been unnecessary – should in the long term have wrecked the programme. It was

Left: One of the last drawings of the P.1150 before this machine was overtaken by the P.1154. Today, almost 20 years later, we are once again drawing similar aircraft with PCB Pegasus engines./*BAe*

Below: One of the early configurations of the P.1154RAF, shown with 300-gal tanks and AS.30 missiles./*BAe*

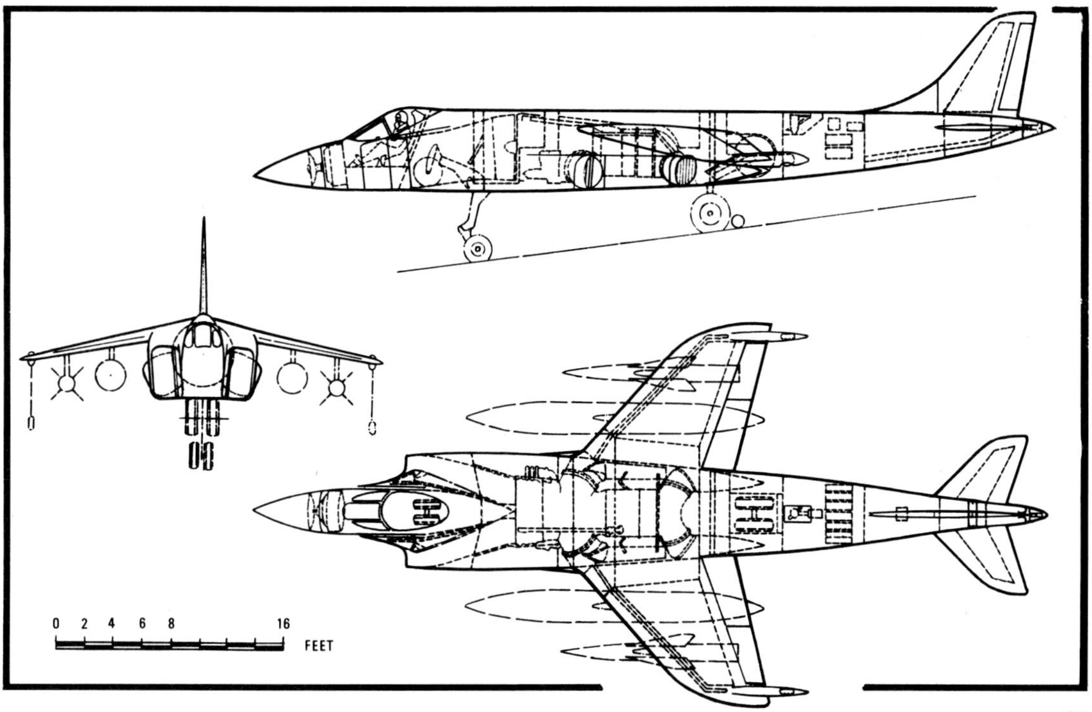

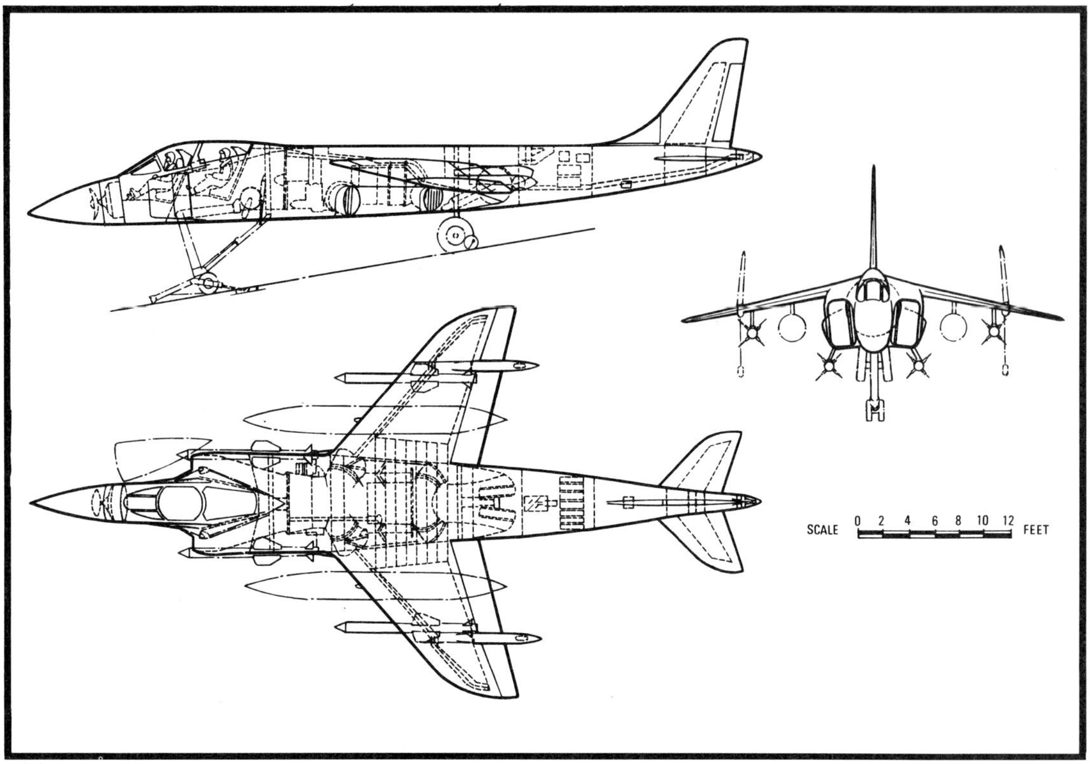
SCALE 0 2 4 6 8 10 12 FEET

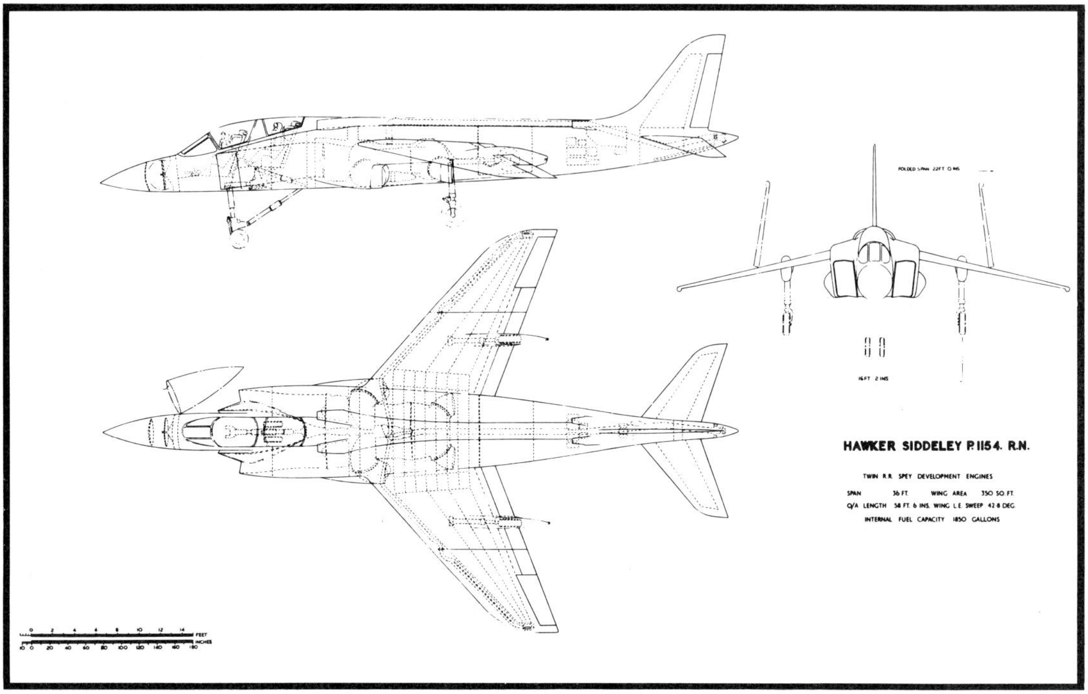
FOLDED SPAN 22 FT. 0 INS
16 FT 2 INS
HAWKER SIDDELEY P.1154. R.N.
TWIN R.R. SPEY DEVELOPMENT ENGINES
SPAN 36 FT. WING AREA 350 SQ. FT.
O/A LENGTH 58 FT. 6 INS. WING L.E. SWEEP 42·8 DEG.
INTERNAL FUEL CAPACITY 1850 GALLONS
FEET
INCHES

Left: The initial P.1154RN was not too much of a departure from the RAF aircraft, though it had greater span and inboard wing landing gear. This September 1963 drawing shows 300-gal tanks and four Red Top missiles./*BAe*

Below left: This drawing shows that by January 1964 the RN aircraft had little commonality with that for the RAF. Immediately evident features include the further extended span, and the longer main gears mounted nearer the fuselage./*BAe*

Above: Model photograph of P.1154RN, in September 1963 form. /*BAe*

stipulated that the nose, wings and tail had to fold, that catapult capability was essential, and that a totally different CW radar was required, with a giant 30-inch dish aerial. This was the last time a British Service failed to see that 'demands' could prove lethal; in fact, even at this early date many Navy staff had become captivated by the idea that had been put to them by Rolls-Royce a few weeks earlier of a Phantom with Spey engines.

Obviously, it should always be possible for a CTOL aircraft to have a better payload/range capability than a V/STOL of equal total installed thrust and the same general level of technology; but, had the Air Warfare team at the Admiralty known that an incoming Labour government would cancel the planned CVA-01 carrier, soon leaving the Royal Navy with no ship able to operate a Phantom or any other high-Mach CTOL aircraft, such arguments would have seemed academic.

This was a pity, because a joint-service P.1154 would have been possible, and there is little doubt the project would not have run into the crippling problems of weight-escalation, engine/inlet mismatch and excessive drag that afflicted that other abortive exercise in commonality, the F-111 (subject of another book in this series). The P.1154 was the first time anyone had really tried to design a multi-role combat aircraft with jet V/STOL capability. It naturally came out much larger, and especially much longer, than the P.1127. The fuselage was 58 feet long, and broad and boxy like those of the later F-14 and F-15. Unlike the P.1127 the engine was removed downwards, leaving the wing undisturbed. Even the BS.100 looked quite small by comparison (whereas the smaller Pegasus looked big in relation to a P.1127) and there was room for 1,200 Imp gallons of fuel internally. For reasons of balance the equipment, such as the comprehensive array of avionics (except the radar), had to be at the rear. There was no way out of the problem, despite the 1,000lb mass of cable looms linking more than 1,500 signal lines over a distance of almost 40 feet. Typical mission loads included four 1,000lb bombs and two 300 Imp gallon drop tanks. Other loads included a reconnaissance pack or four Red Top AAMs. Peak Mach number at height was 1.73.

Down at Patchway Bristol Siddeley had since 1961 risked its own money on advanced steel and titanium parts and in PCB rig testing, though the company got proper cover from the new Ministry of Aviation for the BS.100 (something never offered for the original Pegasus) backed up by MWDP for the PCB studies. A Pegasus 2 ran with PCB in December 1962, the engine being installed on the test-bench inverted so that in the jet-lift mode the glowing jets pointed skywards. This engine was then rebuilt with the so-called 'droop and trail' anhedralled front nozzles, to lead into testing of the BS.100. By 1964 some 135 hours had been run at PCB temperatures up to 1,177°C, with thrust boost of 35 per cent and very stable burning even with massive ingress of water. The first BS.100 ran on 30 October 1964, and development went extremely well. Within two months another engine had passed 30,000lb, with PCB on and nozzles aft. By April 1965 engines 1001 to 1004 had run, and 1005 was bolted together 'finger tight' and placed in storage.

Apart from the Navy, the influence that had the most adverse effect on the programme was Rolls-Royce. In November 1962 the Derby salesmen had been armed with a brochure describing a 7,500lb package comprising twin RB.168 Spey engines with vectoring fan nozzles on the outboard sides only and with a complex cross-over exhaust for the rear pipes so that failure of one engine did not flip the P.1154 on its back. For some reason the Navy liked this: they appeared to think it conferred twin-engine safety, whereas even in the wing-supported mode a landing at 146 knots with either engine out would have pulled out the arrester wire. Engine-failure after take-off, in the jet-lift regime, would have meant immediate ditching, and even loss of an engine later in the mission meant ejection back in the vicinity of the carrier, so one marvelled that this unhelpful proposal lasted for months (and is shown in an accompanying P.1154RN drawing). Throughout 1963 Rolls spread the gospel that the twin-Spey 1154 would be 'cheaper' and 'use a proven engine', but in late March the Ministry selected the BS.100/9 at 35,800lb thrust and asked Rolls to help with development and production. It was to some degree this episode, as much as Bristol Siddeley's tie-up with SNECMA of France on the civil JT9D engine, that resulted in Rolls buying out its rival in 1966.

An idea of how the 1154 went during 1963 is provided by quoting Camm: 'Everything we put up is rejected by either the RAF or the Navy, and sometimes by both'. It seemed the only customer who really tried to make it all happen was Peter Thorneycroft, who was Minister of Aviation in 1960-62 and of Defence in 1962-4. Sadly, he believed, like McNamara in the Pentagon, in the concept of commonality. But, as the two services grew further and further apart in their ideas of how the 1154 should be designed, he appeared to have no pool of impartial and technically literate advisors. In the author's view he should have pressed ahead with all speed from the start with the 1154RAF, which was a firm and viable project which could have yielded production aircraft by the specified year of 1969, if not earlier. Had the Navy realised all it had to do was specify the minimum of change orders, such as a folding nose, it too would soon have got working hardware which by now would have an immense background of ocean operations. Instead of this the Navy thought of as many things as it could to make the 1154RN different.

One change that seemed unavoidable was to throw out bicycle landing gear. Unlike today's Sea Harrier the 1154 was to be cat-launched, and there was no way the twin main wheels could ride over the shuttle on the steam catapult. As deck operation is possible with very high tyre pressures it was possible to use small main wheels and mount them on the wings (in a way studied back in early 1127 days) folding into Tupolev-style fairings. Extra drag was acceptable though the gear pods interfered with the movable surfaces. By January 1964 – when, against all odds, metal was actually cut on the RAF aircraft – the wing had grown even larger. Starting life at 30ft, 4ft greater span than the 1154RAF, it now had to be extended a further 6ft to handle the increased weight, and house 1,850gal of fuel internally. Further work was done on the long two-shock inlets to raise Mach number to about 1.95, at which point the Navy complained because 2 had not been reached. Even Rolls-Royce recognised that if two Speys were used they would have to exceed 15,000lb each. Still the Navy was not interested, and, egged on by the Chief of Defence Staff, Lord Mountbatten, it withdrew in February 1964. Instead it decided to buy 60 Spey-Phantoms for £45 million (it actually got 24 at a cost of £113 million).

Once the Navy had pulled out, the 1154RAF made real progress. When the Labour Government was elected in October 1964 the design was approaching completion, and the first flight prototype was taking shape at Kingston. Tragically, the Labour Party had for its own reasons picked on the British aircraft industry as a political target. It announced that it was desirable to stop British planemaking and buy from the United States. In the case of the TSR.2 the reason given to the public was one of cost-saving, but with

Below: To amuse, or horrify, draughtsmen these are the basic geometric drawings of the jetpipe proposed by Rolls-Royce (Derby) to switch the hot jet from the left engine to the right side of the aircraft and vice versa in the twin-engined P.1154RN./*Rolls-Royce*

Bottom left: This model shows the P.1154RAF in its final form with a long dorsal spine and two pairs of dorsal ram inlets./*BAe*

Bottom: Almost all major airframe parts for the first P.1154 had been finished when the programme was cancelled. This was one of the seven spar frames carrying loads across the top of the fuselage./*BAe*

the P.1154RAF Prime Minister Wilson was advised to tell the public that this Hawker aircraft 'will not be in service in time to serve as a Hunter replacement'. He indicated the Hunters were almost falling apart, and that only the American Phantom would do as a quick replacement. Defence Minister Denis Healey announced that now the RAF would get its Hunter replacement 'four years earlier'.

The P.1154 programme was cancelled on 2 February 1965. The RAF finally got its Phantoms in 1969, at a price considerably greater than the final estimated unit cost of the P.1154RAF. Hunters are still with the RAF, Royal Navy and many other air forces in 1981. But the BS.100 left a valuable legacy of PCB experience.

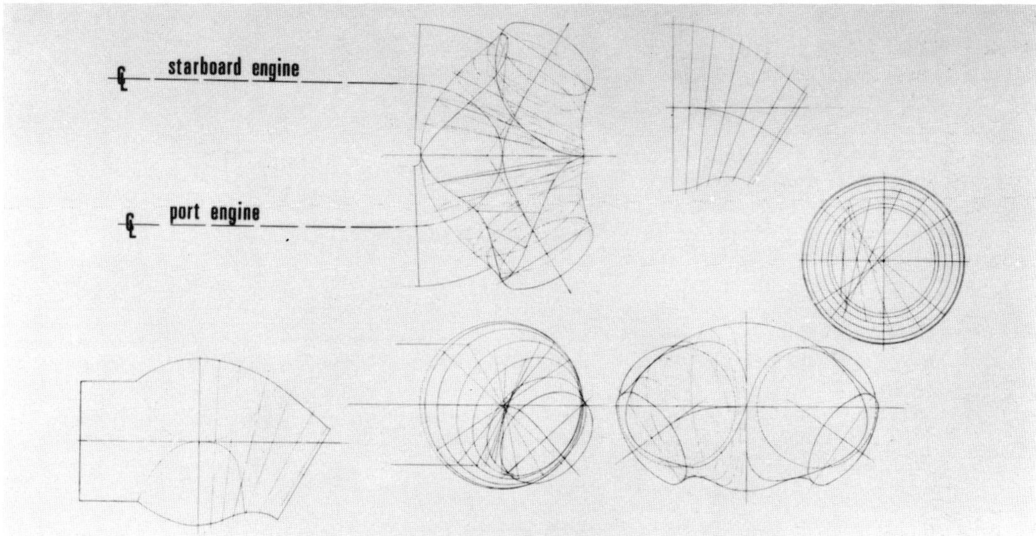

4
The Harrier

When the P.1154 was abruptly cancelled in February 1965 the government did allow Hawker Aircraft to continue to study the smaller, subsonic P.1127 as a possible tactical aircraft for the RAF. This meant that Britain's already considerable effort applied to jet V/STOL had not been entirely wasted, and today, 17 years later, the Harrier has demonstrated that an air force does not have to rely on vulnerable fixed bases. The potential of jet V/STOL is so large that even today most air staffs take the easy way out by leaving it to others, but these are arguments best left to later in this book. For the moment, it is appropriate to take a long look at the situation in 1965.

Though in the preceding chapter I criticised NATO by calling the NBMR-3 competition a bandwagon, and a house of cards, in fact had NATO not existed the P.1127 could well have withered away in the bleak climate in Britain. On the one hand Hawker and Bristol Siddeley were faced with an official defence policy strongly influenced by the belief that any kind of manned combat aircraft was a non-starter; despite the throbbing production lines of MiGs, Mirages, Starfighters and Phantoms, such things were supposed (in Britain, at least) to disappear from the sky. On the other they found an Air Staff which, instead of grabbing at the P.1127 as not just a straw to keep them afloat but a very new straw of open-ended and largely undiscovered possibilities, instead poured scorn on it as small, subsonic and hardly worth serious consideration. While in the United States the Navy was planning to take a near-Mach 2 aircraft, the F-8, and turn it into a subsonic aircraft in order to do a superior job in tactical attack missions, in London the official view was that if it didn't have swing wings and highly supersonic speed it was not worth bothering about. The posture was intensified by suggestions from the Hawker Siddeley Group that it might be worth the RAF taking another look at the Buccaneer; it was to be another five years before Hawker Siddeley, as foster-parent to the RAF Spey-Phantom, discovered that with a typical bomb load the despised subsonic Buccaneer was faster than the Phantom, and burned fuel at half the rate.

This polarisation on Mach 2 adversely influenced all the P.1127/Kestrel studies that had continued throughout the lifetime of the supersonic P.1150 and 1154. Some of these studies had been at company level with Northrop, for example, and others at government level with the USA, Federal Germany and Italy. NASA, as an instrument of the US government, had maintained the closest ties with Kingston and Dunsfold, where its engineers and test pilots learned all they could about jet V/STOL. But the home air force never showed any public interest in the P.1127 or its successors. When he was appointed Minister of Defence, Peter Thorneycroft visited Dunsfold and showed polite interest in the Hawker accomplishments. Nearly three years later Sir Roy Dobson commented 'I thought there would be an order for a wing of P.1127s so that the services could get used to VTO. Absolutely nothing happened.' A former Chief of the Defence Staff, Sir William Dickson, privately criticised *Flight International*, which had written 'It is lamentable that the RAF did not long ago ask for 50 or so of the straightforward P.1127, so that by now some practical experience and potential export sales might have been achieved'; he said 'The Press ought to be told that such a machine is a toy, and quite useless for operational purposes'. One of his successors, however, Sir Thomas Pike, had been appointed Chief of the Air Staff in 1960, and he had brought a welcome breath of common sense objectivity. He had never subscribed to the Sandys 'no more manned aircraft' doctrine, and throughout the NATO NBMR-3 ballyhoo had quietly satisfied himself that Hawker and Bristol Siddeley had a fallback 'improved P.1127' programme based on the Pegasus. The crucial question, however, was how far to push the idea of an improved P.1127 which could only compete with the 1154.

It was the election of a Labour government that provided the answer in October 1964. Breathing hatred against the British aircraft industry, which they called 'overgrown and mentally retarded children', the politicians wanted big projects to be publicly seen to be killed off. The bitter struggle between Rolls-Royce and Bristol Siddeley, and between the Royal Navy and RAF, had made the

Above right: The basic layout of the Harrier is unique but logical and has never been regretted, though the wing has to be above the engine and the avionics racking is at the tail./*BAe*

Right: Three-view of the Harrier as originally designed, prior to addition of LRMTS and RWR./*BAe*

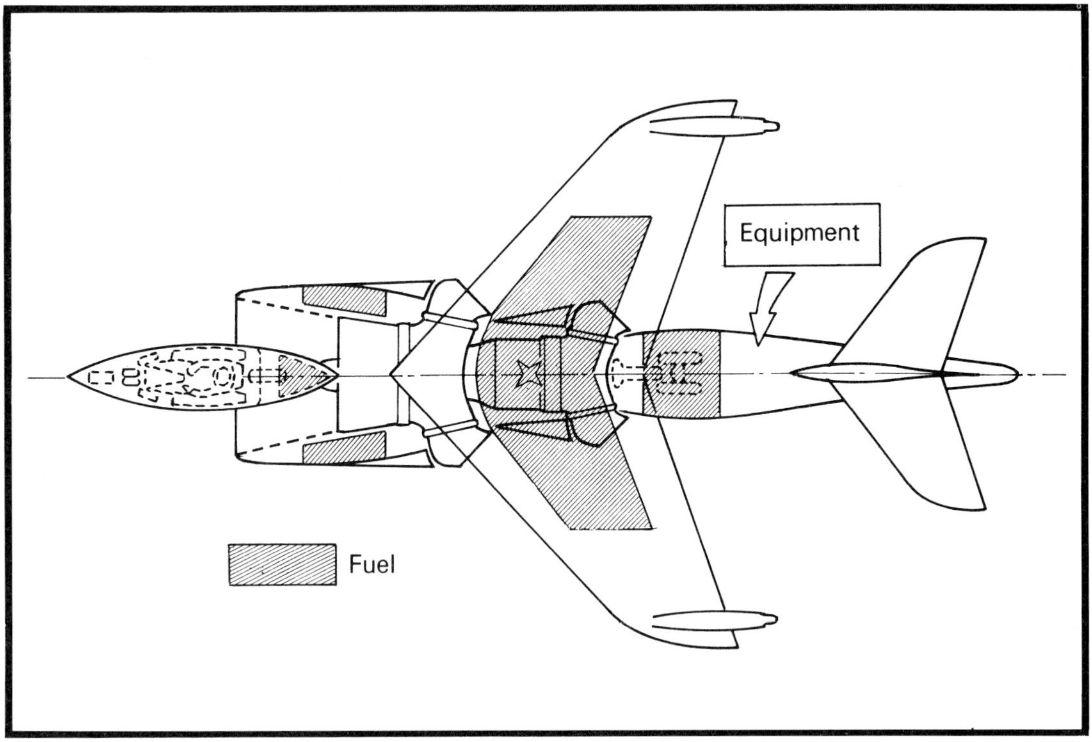
Equipment
Fuel

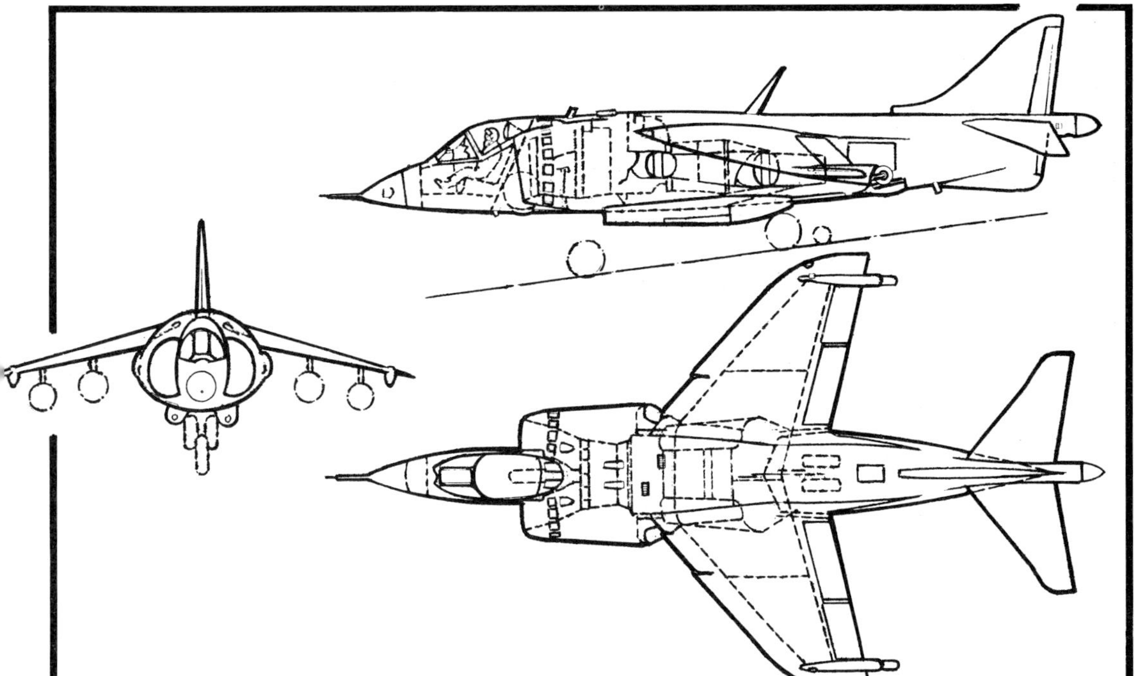

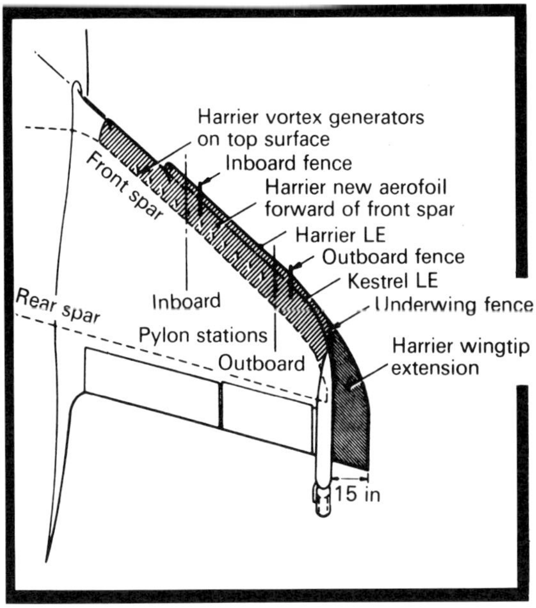

Above: The Harrier wing retained the Kestrel's peaky pressure distribution with a large nose radius, but the wing was largely new and had extra area outboard, which meant at the rear./*BAe*

Below: XV276, the first P.1127RAF, before its first flight in August 1966. Note the six-door inlet./*BAe*

Below right: Features of the Pegasus as used in all aircraft of the Harrier family to date./*Rolls-Royce*

1154 programme an obvious target. It took patient missionary work by Tom Pike and his 1963 successor, Sir Charles Elworthy, to ensure that, when the 1154 died, an 'improved 1127' should be allowed to continue. Even this crumb was not easily won, and it required rewriting the terms on which government funding was to be allowed for aircraft research which, even in the case of the TSR.2 and HS.681, had previously demanded the existence of a related civil application! Even so, Prime Minister Wilson's government refused to sanction an actual go-ahead on an improved P.1127 as a production aircraft. The most that could be won was that the government acknowledged, for the first time, RAF interest in an aircraft derived from the P.1127 and powered by a Pegasus engine, and agreed to fund a small batch of development aircraft.

The way Mr Wilson announced it, immediately after terminating the P.1154RAF on 2 February 1965, was 'We believe that there is an urgent need for an operational version of the P.1127. As soon as it can be negotiated, a contract will be placed for a limited development programme so that the RAF can have, by the time they need it, an aircraft which will in fact be the first in the field, with vertical takeoff for close support of our land forces . . . We are also going into the question of further research and development into this to see whether it can be boosted into something much more substantial.' The last statement, which appeared to suggest carrying on where the P.1150 left off, has never been explained.

By this time Sir Sydney Camm was beginning

slowly to hand over the reins at Kingston. He passed peacefully away on his local golf course in March 1966, and so, like Mitchell with the Spitfire, did not live to see the 1127 reach maturity. The original P.1127 had been drafted mainly by Ralph Hooper, but it was to be Yorkshire-born John Fozard who was to become so synonymous with Hawker Siddeley's future V/STOL tactical aircraft that he was to become popularly 'Mr Harrier'. Previously a Blackburn apprentice, he had worked his way up at Kingston to become Chief Designer, P.1154, and then Chief Designer, P.1127RAF. Subsequently, thanks to his extraordinary ability to communicate, he was lost to the design side and became a salesman, his present title being Marketing Director, Kingston/Brough Division. His description of what happened in February 1965, voiced a few months afterwards was 'The Men from the Ministry – which I believe they now call Mintech – came down and said "You must stop making the 1154; but you can take some of the nav/attack system out of the 1154 and try and fit it in the 1127, with an uprated engine. Then we might buy it for the RAF".'

In this strange way was born the P.1127RAF, which two years later was to be named Harrier. The name had originally been selected by the RAF for the P.1154, and back in 1927 had been borne by a Hawker biplane bomber powered by a much earlier Bristol engine, the Jupiter.

The Mintech (Ministry of Technology) contract for six P.1127RAF development aircraft (XV276-281) came through with remarkable speed, on 19 February, barely two weeks after the termination of the 1154RAF. Only a draft Operational Requirement existed, and so Hawker Aircraft had at first to guess what the 1127RAF would have to carry. They also had to take some quick and far-reaching decisions on how far they could redesign the airframe, compared with the Kestrel, without compromising the timing. They got strong signals that this was to be a quick, cheap, troublefree exercise; as far as possible the idea was literally to take the 'black boxes' out of the 1154RAF and pack them, along with a more powerful Pegasus engine, into the existing airframe of the Kestrel. But it could not really be so simple.

The Kestrel had never been planned as a definitive RAF aircraft for possible large-scale long-term use, but as a vehicle with which the three participating nations could play with jet V/STOL. The mismatch between the engine thrust centre and aircraft cg had been rectified, and stability at low speeds had been improved in a last-minute modification which extended the tailplane span from 12 feet to nearly 14 feet to catch a useful sidewash flow. But despite this the increased engine power, especially in low-angle wingborne flight, caused powerful destabilising effects, and the Kestrel became known as 'the most delightful-to-fly unstable fighter'! It was in no way dangerous, if the pilot kept alert and followed the book, and was far superior to any other V/STOL of the time; but in February 1965 the Kingston team appreciated better than anyone that an even higher standard would be necessary for a regular operational V/STOL aircraft.

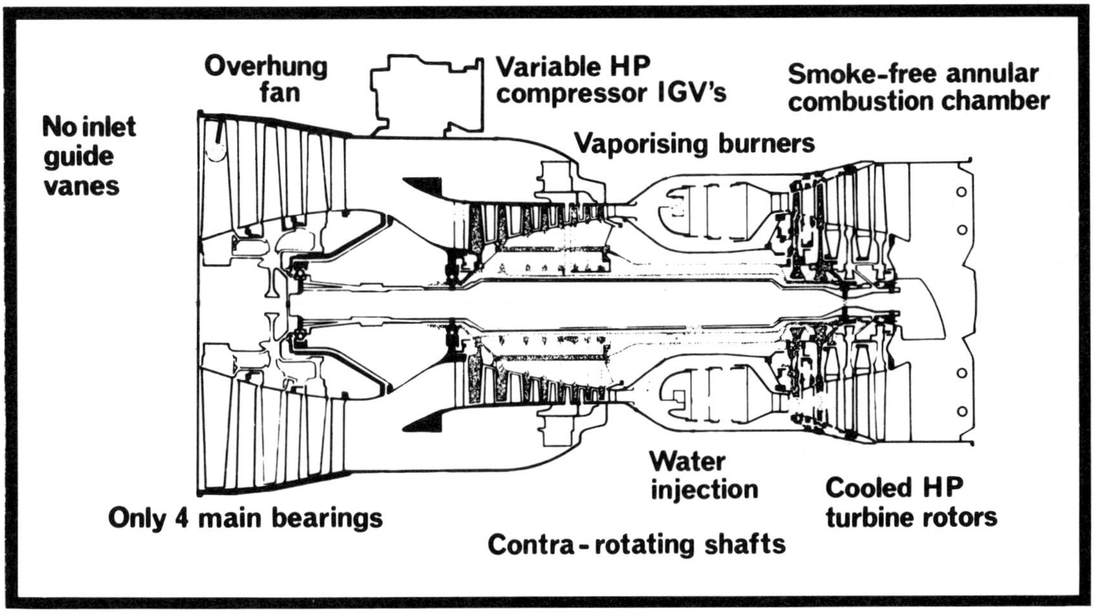

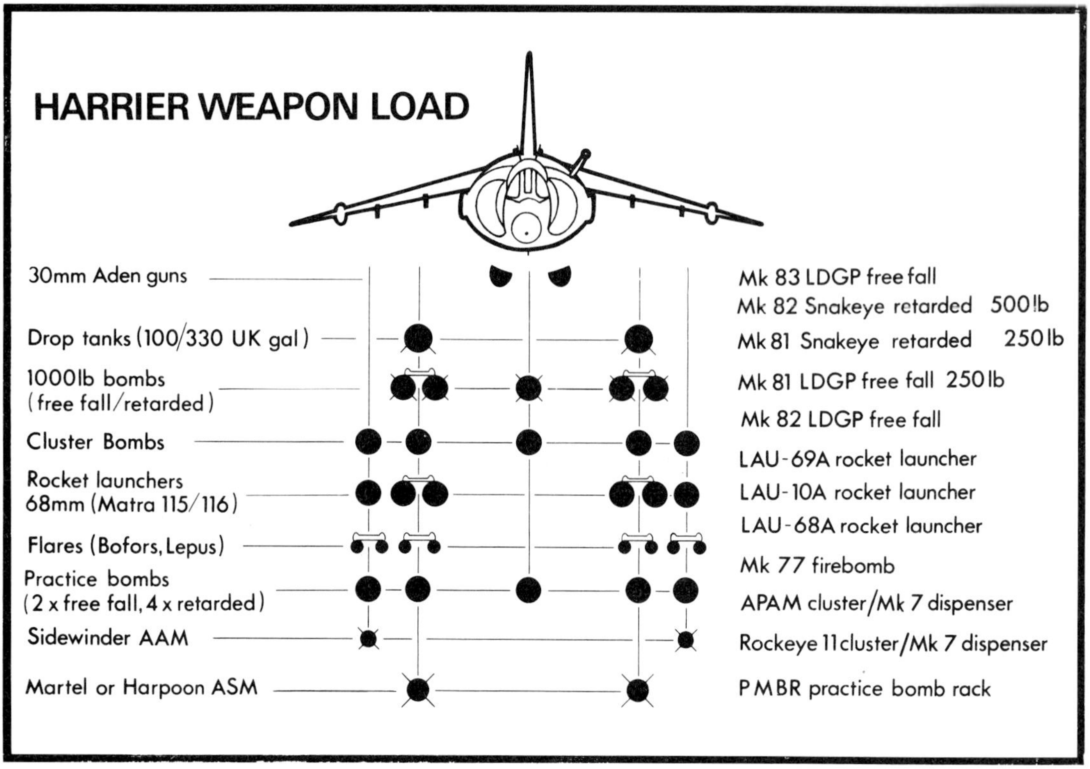

This was despite the fact that, thanks to the Pegasus 6, thrust was to increase by a further 25 per cent. A further problem was that the essential extended-span tailplane suffered alarming vibrations when the engine was run at high power on the ground with nozzles pointing aft, the turbulent shear surrounding the hot jets causing oscillations of about 6 inches amplitude with frequency 13 cycles per second! The Kestrel TES had to be issued with special ground-anchored dampers bolted to each tailplane during ground running in order to meet the required 1,000hr life. Another basic shortcoming was that from the original P.1127 the landing gear had been barely acceptable, the root cause being freedom in roll. This had made manoeuvring at high speed on the ground difficult if not dangerous, and threatened to break the fragile outrigger legs. There were many other problems, not the least being the wish to clear the forthcoming P.1127RAF to carry heavier or bulkier stores in the course of time when even more power might be available.

It was obvious to the Kingston engineers that they were faced with a major task, not just finding where to put the black boxes but virtually in starting from scratch and creating a new aircraft. While they got down to it under high pressure – and do not forget the emotional stress of planemaking, in which designers who have lived for years with ulcer-making problems (for example, trying to achieve a P.1154 variable inlet acceptable to both the RAF and RN) suddenly have to forget all about them and apply themselves round-the-clock on the next project – the officials tried to produce an OR. The only document to go on was the most recent draft of OR.356 (1154RAF), and in the end this was merely reissued but with the mission numerical values down-graded to suit the expected capability of the 1127RAF. As far as possible there were no changes; the only significant down-grading concerned level flight Mach number and mission payload/range. Another factor not insisted upon was the radar, which clearly would call for a new forward fuselage. Mating the complete 1154RAF forward fuselage and cockpit with the 1127RAF fuselage was impossible. The primary mission was to be close support, and little was said for the moment about air-to-air missions, so radar was accorded a low priority. In any case this was the least-developed of all 1154RAF avionics (Ferranti, the final winner, never received the full development contract) and this was the only major avionics item from the 1154RAF not to be continued.

For the moment the chief objectives appeared to be

the following: to maintain the correct relationship between thrust centre and cg in hovering flight; provide adequate pitch stability over the complete flight envelope with external stores; ensure good handling from about minus 50 knots up to 635 knots or Mach 1.25; remove all concern for tailplane fatigue life; and redesign the structure for arduous use from unprecedentedly austere bases (eg a clearing in a forest) for a design life of 15,000 hours. A parallel effort redesigned virtually the entire systems to minimise maintenance problems in the same harsh forward-base environment.

Thanks to the repositioning of the engine in the Kestrel, the Pegasus 6 could remain in the same longitudinal position in the 1127RAF despite its much greater thrust and a rearwards movement of its thrust centre; the latter was still well forward of the aft stability limit. On the other hand the designers were concerned at possible degradation in stability in conventional flight, and took pains to prevent a rearwards shift of cg across the wing chord. Today the inherently unstable fighter is a specific design objective, under what has become known as control-configured vehicle (CCV) technology, the deficiency being rectified by high-authority and extremely reliable black boxes. In early 1965 CCV was a dark art that had not yet been practised, and it was deemed prudent to shift the aerodynamic centre aft to take care of the worst case with external stores.

There was in the early jet-V/STOL era a general consensus that the wing should be sized to the high-speed cruise, as was done with the Martin Marauder of 1939. Today the general view is that the extra weight and drag of a larger wing is worth having, to improve overload STOL takeoff, cruise efficiency and especially the ability to pull g in air combat. This is despite the fact that for low-level high-speed attack missions the wing should have the smallest possible span and area. On top of this, today we have extremely efficient wing profiles with a flattish top and bulged underside, known as sonic roof-top or supercritical sections. These can be of great benefit to almost all high-subsonic aircraft (though they may slightly reduce the Mach number reached in a dive), and are a feature of the next-generation AV-8B described later. In 1965, however, the Kingston team adhered to the NPL-developed 'peaky' section profile, though with a generous nose radius, and to a

Left: This listing of weapon loads does not quite tally with the diagram but shows UK stores on the left and US stores on the right./*BAe*

Below: Mission equipment in the RAF Harrier, which except for the laser LRMTS is duplicated in the two-seater. Not shown are the peripherals such as the RWR and post-attack camera./*BAe*

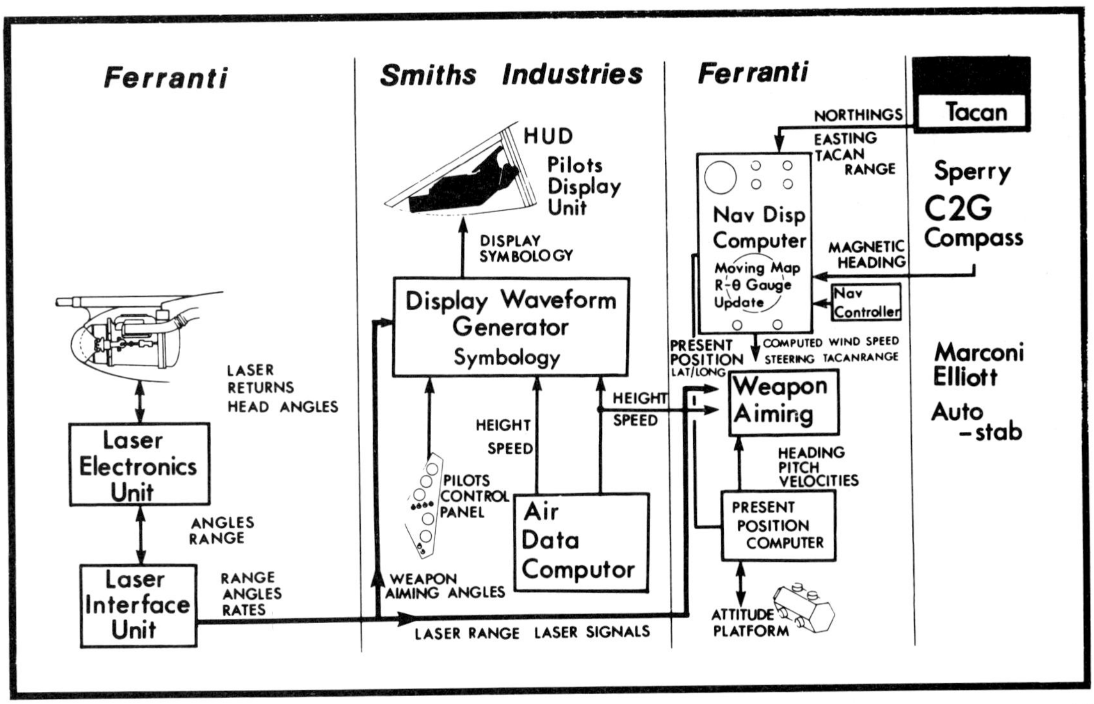

wing of small span and area. Thickness/chord ratio varied from 10% at the root to 5 at the tip.

Compared with the Kestrel the leading edge was redesigned with a dogtooth, extended outer chord and a curving streamwise tip extending 15 inches beyond the outrigger fairing. This provided the required rearwards shift in aerodynamic centre considered necessary. A row of 12 vortex generators was provided at about 12% chord, and care was taken to grade the spanwise loadings to ensure that, in transonic flight, there was a smooth and progressive breakdown of flow across the upper surface. In addition the wing was stressed for four pylons, rated at 1,200lb inboard and 650lb outboard, and of course cleared for the much longer operational life of 3,000 hours in the low close-support mission (which meant demonstrating 15,000 hours). Overall, the result was most successful. Though in wing-supported flight with external stores the destabilising effects of over 30,000 jet horsepower passing just below the tailplane led to unusual and slightly hair-raising trim curves, there is never a pilot problem. Even at AOA (angle of attack) as high as 20°, pitch stability is adequate under all conditions, which cannot be said of some conventional combat aircraft. The Boscombe handling report recorded 'The almost imperceptible effect on handling throughout the flight envelope of the numerous combinations of stores makes the Harrier a remarkable aircraft.' To master the tailplane problem and allow unrestricted ground running at full power with nozzles aft, without the need for vibration dampers, called for a cautious redesign of the structure. There was no need to change the shape beyond the extended-span kinked type finally adopted for the Kestrel, with 15° anhedral (compared with 0° on the first P.1127 and 18° on subsequent 1127s), but the whole structure was strengthened and emerged at a weight of 203lb, 24lb heavier than the final Kestrel tailplane. This did not quite give the required life of 15,000 demonstrated (simulated) hours, but a second stage of redesign, adding a mere 8lb, comfortably accomplished this goal.

More detailed analysis was needed to cure the weak and spongy nosewheel steering and unacceptable heel-over in fast turns on the ground. Redesigned for the Kestrel, the landing gear steered better and had strengthened outrigger legs, but basic problems such as roll freedom remained. Redesigned again in 1965, the main and nose oleos were dramatically increased in energy absorption, and nosewheel steering was greatly improved; but the heel problem actually worsened, the roll freedom increasing from 1½° to 3½°. Only the much better standard of V/STOL flight control (mentioned later) made the early Harrier acceptable.

The breakthrough came in 1967 when the pre-load in the main (rear centreline) oleo was removed, in a modification called the 'self-shortening' main leg. On reaching the ground on landing, the main leg offers no resistance until it has compressed almost 7 inches, by which time the outriggers are bearing a substantial part of the weight. This transformed the landing gear behaviour. In an official report, 'In VTO the aircraft rides level laterally until thrust exceeds weight, when it unsticks cleanly without abnormal use of lateral control. In conventional or part-jet-borne landings the aircraft settles down level and square immediately on first ground contact, and runs straight and true with no pilot input – indeed, without the need to kick-off drift in crosswinds exceeding 25 knots'. The resulting gear is superior to normal tricycle gears in operation from runways, and because of the four-point support with roughly equal fore/aft weight distribution is ideally suited to V/STOL operation from rough unprepared sites and to the requirement of minimum residual pitch rate on exit from a ski jump.

One problem not mentioned earlier concerned the engine air inlets. Obviously a jet V/STOL has to have the highest possible inlet efficiency in V/STOL and hovering flight, and in the original P.1127 this was so over-riding that a bulbous metal intake was fitted that would have ruined performance in conventional flight. In 1962 an inflatable rubber lip was fitted, but this rippled in high-speed flight despite hold-down suction, and was rapidly torn to pieces. The Kestrel managed with a metal lip offering a compromise between the demands of hovering and forwards flight, but in the latter mode suffered from excessive spillage drag. The Harrier had to have a much better inlet, and one capable of handling not only the greater airflow of the Pegasus 6 but also further increases in airflow demanded by a still more powerful Pegasus that was in prospect.

For the DB (development batch) aircraft the answer was an enlarged inlet incorporating simple mechanical variable geometry. The throat was reshaped, while being kept as short as possible (overlong inlets must be one of the inherent problems of the US Navy XFV-12A) to reduce not only weight but the destabilizing moments in pitch and yaw of the large airflow. The fixed metal cowl lip was profiled to minimise spillage drag, with the same peaky section as the wing, and to generate weakened and delayed shocks at transonic speeds. The boundary-layer bleed door on the cockpit sidewall, introduced on the Kestrel, was enlarged and refined to cope with drag and distortion in forward flight. To maximise pressure recovery in hovering flight six auxiliary inlets were arranged round the cowl, with inner and outer blow-in doors. Though obviously advantageous,

Above: The last P.1127RAF was almost indistinguishable from the initial build-standard of the Harrier GR.1. It is pictured at Boscombe with four pylons and gunpacks./*MoD*

these doors distorted the airflow in the duct to reduce total pressure recovery, and further losses arose on the inner face, around the engine bullet fairing, due mainly to the outflow from the air-conditioning heat-exchanger. Just as drawings were being sealed for production of the Harrier in 1966 a more efficient inlet was completed, the result of patient refinement. It provides better efficiency at the mass-flow of today's Pegasus 11 than did the six-door inlet with the Pegasus 6, though the only externally obvious change is that there are now eight doors round each cowl, and the doors are larger. Today's engine is surge-free over a range of inlet airflow angles and throttle rates that are approached by few conventional fighters, quite apart from having to meet the totally contrasting demands of jet V/STOL.

Probably the most crucial of the functioning airframe components are the vectoring engine nozzles and the RCV (reaction control valve) jets. All are given the status of primary flight controls, and as they are normally used at speeds at which the wing cannot support the aircraft, at heights high enough to be dangerous yet too low to give the pilot much time in an emergency, their authority and reliability has to be as high as any component ever designed.

It seems logical that the four main nozzles should be part of the engine, but from the start of BE.53/2 design they have been mounted on the aircraft. Cantilevered off the engine they would buckle the Pegasus casing or result in considerably greater engine weight. The most essential requirement is that all four, the two front 'cold' nozzles and the rear jet nozzles, should always remain synchronized. All four are ganged together mechanically by a system of rotary shafts, bevel gears, drive gears and drive chains passing round the nozzles. The system is driven by dual motors running on engine bleed air. If either motor fails, the other drives at half speed. Should any nozzle jam, a shear neck in the shafting fails and the nozzles remain locked. Each nozzle runs in an angular-contact ball bearing filled with balls, intermediate balls being smaller than the others and thus able to run in the reverse direction to eliminate friction caused by ball-rubbing. The system has an outstanding history, with not one dangerous failure. Few refinements have been needed, despite the later clearance for Viffing (vectoring in forward flight, described later) at high indicated airspeeds.

The last major area worth mentioning concerns the flight control and RCV system, where the main task was one of refinement. The prime system contractor for the aerodynamic flight controls see-sawed between Fairey and Dowty on the Hunter (Fairey), P.1121 (Dowty), P.1127 (half Fairey, half Dowty), Kestrel (Dowty) and P.1154 (Fairey). The last programme was of little commercial benefit to Fairey, so it was only justice that the company's excellent proposal won the Harrier programme. Auto-stabilization was provided in the 1127RAF, with low authority on pitch and roll only. Later the yaw axis was added, but the autostab remains a simple monoplex circuit.

As noted earlier, a major change in the early 1127 was to switch to stainless pipe handling hot HP bleed air for the RCVs. Each 1 lb/sec of RCV airflow cuts about 70lb off the engine thrust, so the pilot keeps the stick centred whenever he can. In any case, the RCV system is sensitive, and one of the problems encountered by the US Marine Corps (Ch 6) was that helicopter pilots find the Harrier a handful unless they have also previously been fighter pilots. Each RCV is a simple convergent nozzle around which is a swinging shutter driven by the nearby aileron, tailplane or rudder. Roll control is provided by a nozzle at the front of each outrigger fairing; there is a pitch nozzle at each end of the fuselage, and the rear RCV pipe also feeds left/right yaw nozzles. The nozzles are not on/off but have their area, and thus thrust, varied according to stick or pedal position. The roll nozzles have cunning shutters which swing out, to open the nozzle to blast downwards and give upthrust, or inwards to direct the air round the outer side of the nozzle and blast upwards. The roll control was found to be especially crucial, and much work was needed to achieve the correct high sensitivity and 'gearing' (angular acceleration in roll per unit sideways stick displacement). Even without autostab, prolonged hovering is not tiring, and gusts are much less troublesome than with a helicopter because of the

Harrier's high density of over 25lb/cu ft.

All this and many other tasks had to be done to turn a limited short-life trials machine into a weapon fit for squadron pilots. I have not mentioned avionics and weapons, and these were mainly conspicuous by their absence in the first 1127RAF, XV276, when it was flown by Bill Bedford on 31 August 1966. This was the due date, and the aircraft was cleared only after a round-the-clock hustle for a hover at dusk.

Subsequent development not only refined the 1127RAF, named Harrier in early 1967, but added the black boxes and weapons. No requirement existed to change the forward fuselage and cockpit, compared with the Kestrel, and the canopy, mounted on acutely sloping rails to slide diagonally up and to the rear, remained flush with the top of the fuselage downstream. This gives minimum drag for low-level attack, but for an air-combat dogfighter a raised canopy giving all-round pilot view is preferred (and is a feature of the Sea Harrier). On the other hand the small drag of an optically flat windscreen was accepted because, no matter what black boxes may be carried, the bad-weather attack mission demands excellent forward optics and a birdproof screen. The seat, a Martin-Baker 6HA in the Kestrel, was replaced by a zero/zero (ground level at zero airspeed) seat of higher performance with trajectory reaching 300 feet and able to overcome 50 ft/s sink. Designated Mk 9A or 9D, it is fired only by a seat-pan handle, and with rocket assistance is wholly automatic in operation. Once triggered, the ejection sequence blows the canopy by firing the MDC (miniature detonating cord, sometimes visible as a thin white jagged line), fires the seat and then expels the occupant.

There remain only the avionic fit and weapons to round off the outline of the original RAF Harrier. A central item is the FE.541 INAS (inertial nav/attack system), the contractor for which was Ferranti. This company, the original pioneer of the gyro gunsight and famous for airborne radar (such as that for the 1154RAF), was – together with Elliott Brothers and English Electric, both swallowed by the GEC/Marconi empire – a British pioneer of inertial guidance systems which can accurately steer a vehicle without external aids. INAS was designed around 1961 for the NBMR-3 programme and is thus older than the system fitted to the RAF Jaguar. Significantly, neither aircraft was at first fitted with radar, both were later given a laser ranger, and both were later offered with various radar fits, one of which is standard in the Sea Harrier.

Heart of INAS is the inertial platform, mounted in the nose and bolted to the forward pressure bulkhead. This forms the core of the IMS (inertial measuring system) together with the present-position computer in the avionics bay in the rear fuselage and the nav control box in the cockpit. The IMS feeds the largest avionic item, the nav display and computer, which forms the central feature in the panel in front of the pilot. The NDC's central display is a projected topographic map; each map, loaded as a 35mm cassette, covers about 800 nautical miles north/south and 900 east/west. Present position appears at the centre, and the pilot can crank in destination or waypoint buttons and other data such as offset position. Other information is fed from the Sperry compass and Tacan, while the pilot's left hand falls conveniently on the pistol-grip hand controller, to the rear of the throttle quadrant, which incorporates a rolling-ball input and a white 'fix' button depressed as the aircraft overflies a point whose position must be recalled or automatically regained.

In action the pilot uses not only the NDC, which forms the head-down display (HDD), but to an even greater extent looks ahead through the head-up display (HUD) on which bright symbology gives him navigation, steering, weapon-delivery and other information. The Harrier HUD was one of the first such units in production; it was created by a young company called Specto which was gobbled up by the competition (Smiths Industries). To complete the original INAS, Ferranti supplied the weapon-aiming computer and a ballistics box in which, before each mission, slide-in plugs are inserted. One plug, normally fixed in place, handles gunfiring; three other plugs can be inserted, each inputting the ballistic characteristics of a particular type of free-fall weapon. The pilot has to check that he has the correct plugs for the actual weapons hung on the pylons, and then select the correct pylon(s) before making an attack.

The avionic kit of the original RAF Harrier was completed by such radio navaids as Tacan, UHF homing and IFF, and by communications such as

VHF, tactical VHF frequencies and UHF. An F95 70mm camera was fitted in the nose, looking obliquely sideways for post-attack use, and a HUD recording camera.

No inbuilt armament was specified. Instead the operational load is hung on seven pylons, two of which on the left and right sides of the fuselage belly are normally occupied by gun pods each housing an Aden Mk 4 cannon of 30mm calibre with 130 rounds of ammunition. If removed, these pods are replaced by axial strakes which like the gun pods increase pressure on the underside of the fuselage when hovering near the ground. (As related later, much more is now being done to improve flows and pressure distributions round the aircraft in low-altitude hovering.) Other weapons and tanks are listed in an accompanying diagram. Like the inboard wing pylons, the centreline hardpoint is rated at 1,200lb, though it is possible to fly with an external load exceeding 5,000lb and a production aircraft (in USMC markings but actually XV742) demonstrated an external weapon load of 8,000lb in 1973.

A total of 630gal (757 US gal, 2,864 litres, 5,040lb) of fuel is housed in five integral tanks in the fuselage and two in the wings. This can be supplemented by two 330gal ferry tanks or two jettisonable 100gal combat tanks. Only the wing points are plumbed for drop tanks, and in accord with the eventual specification a refuelling pipe was run to the top of the left inlet cowl to which can be attached a long inclined flight-refuelling probe with the tip above and ahead of the pilot on the left side.

In the next chapter an outline is given of how the Harrier developed for the RAF. Included are details of subsequent modifications, including the tandem-seat dual variant.

Above: XV739 and 742 on trials from Boscombe, the latter having the five-camera reconnaissance pod as well as flanking gun packs. /*BAe*

Below: Locations of mission equipment as agreed at the start of the P.1127RAF production programme. Tactical VHF was not fitted, but today Harriers have a laser nose and front/rear radar warning aerials at the tail./*BAe*

Below left: Another item not normally carried in RAF service is self-defence Sidewinders, but the AIM-9B version was cleared for use in early trials from Boscombe./*BAe*

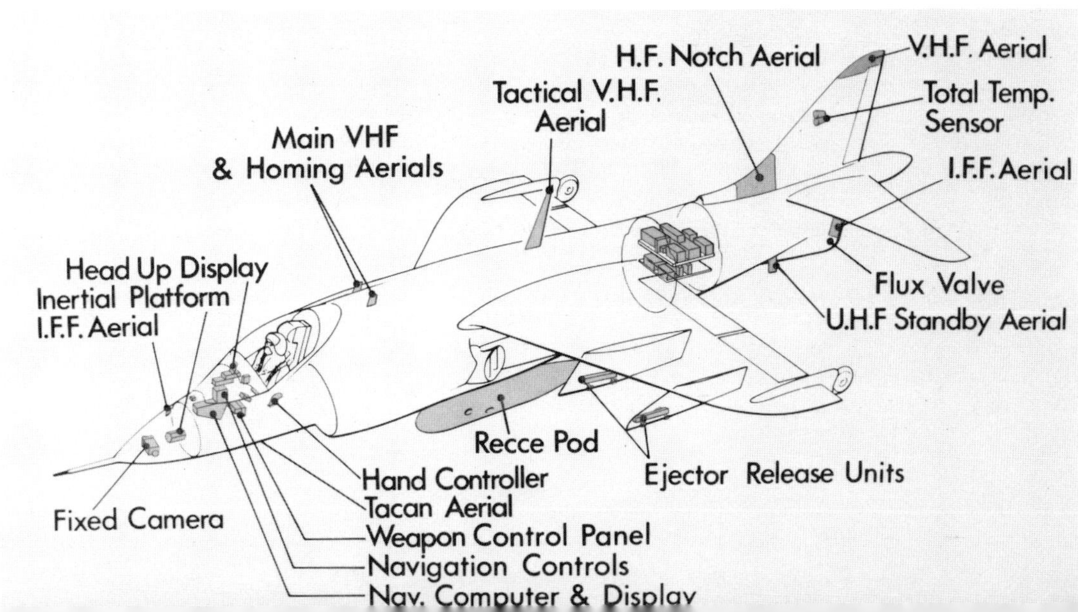

5
RAF Service

Whereas the official view in February 1965 was that the government was merely prepared to look at the 'P.1127RAF' and later take a decision on procurement, it was soon evident that this was a mere political posture. Without waiting for any flight-test results, the drafting of a production contract began in February 1966, and at the Hanover show three months later the Hawker Siddeley Group had been advised it would shortly receive an ITP (instruction to proceed) on long-lead materials and parts. Production tooling was already being manufactured. Go-ahead on production was signalled in late 1966, and in early 1967 the first contract was received, for 60 single-seaters designated Harrier GR.1 (GR for ground attack and reconnaissance). A second contract followed for two prototype and eight production two-seaters designated Harrier T.2. The two-seater is described later.

Initial flight development of the six P.1127RAF aircraft served chiefly to confirm that this was already a mature aircraft. No major difficulty was encountered, and most of the effort was applied to such routine matters as perfecting the flight-control handling, adding and debugging the avionics, and developing the engine and its control system. The P.1127 policy of making the aircraft easily flyable without autostabilisation was continued, so it remained vital to achieve exceptionally fast and accurate pilot control of engine thrust. By 1970 the Pegasus 6, by this time in service as the Pegasus 101, could unfailingly be slammed from 55 to 100 per cent rpm in just 2.5 seconds. At the same time rpm and jet-pipe temperature were automatically limited, and further development was undertaken to perfect the relationship between throttle-lever position and power at the upper end of the scale in the hovering regime. As originally developed on P.1127s, the power curve rises sharply in the cruise range and then, near the thrust required for hovering flight, a different relationship is established giving about 0.1g vertical acceleration per inch of lever travel. Of course, nozzle movement also has to be fast and lag-free; little further development was required for this vital system, which from the start offered vectoring rates up to 90°/sec.

Much more effort was needed on the avionics, especially the nav/attack INAS. It was well worthwhile, and six months after an integrated example began flying in early 1967 the system gave an accuracy in navigation (root-mean-square, with no updating) of only a little greater than 1 nautical mile error per hour of flight. Ferranti claimed this to be 'twice as good as that achieved by any other strike aircraft', such as the F-104G. In a blind first-pass attack, in other words a single run over a target of known position achieved purely on the INAS guidance, the weapon-delivery accuracy proved to be seldom worse than 6 mils (milliradians angular error), again an excellent result. Later, as outlined in this chapter, attack accuracy was improved by a laser nose.

All six development aircraft flew by August 1967, by which time the concept of the tactical V/STOL aircraft had been made even more obvious by the destruction of Arab airpower in the Six-Day war, and somewhat more acceptable by the demonstration at Domodedovo of a Russian vectored-thrust research aircraft. Soon after it had flown, the last development aircraft was ferried non-stop to Rome by the chief test pilot, Duncan Simpson, making a vertical landing. It went on to complete tropical trials at Sigonella, Sicily. Two months later, in October 1967, Merewether took a sister aircraft out to the Mediterranean and flew VTOLs from the helicopter platform of the anchored cruiser *Andrea Doria*. This was by no means the first Hawker V/STOL at sea, but the platform of this cruiser measures just 92.5 by 52.5 feet! Other shipboard experience is outlined in the chapter on the Sea Harrier.

Duncan Simpson flew XV738, the first production GR.1, on 28 December 1967. A particularly noisy day at Dunsfold followed early in the new year when the

Above right: No 1 Squadron photographed at Wittering in April 1971, two years after the unit had become the first in the world to be operational with jet V/STOL. The photograph is modelled on a famous picture of the same squadron taken exactly 53 years earlier when it was fighting in France with the S.E.5a./*Richard Wilson*

Right: On-airfield chores in 1971 included using a self-powered loader to hoist Matra 155 launchers containing 19 SNEB rockets of 68 mm calibre./*MoD*

M

Above: XV748 in its element, pulling g at about Mach 0.95 just over the treetops. Note the white shock haze above the wings./*BAe*

Above right: A simplified cutaway of the Harrier GR.3 with LRMTS and RWR fitted but without guns./*BAe*

Left: John Farley, Dunsfold chief test pilot, and John Fozard, former chief designer and now divisional marketing director, celebrate the first Sea Harrier ski launch at Farnborough with a bottle of après-ski champagne, August 1978./*BAe*

Below: Pupil, in front cockpit, and instructor in a T.4 of No 233 OCU, showing the backseater's separate windscreen and side-hinged canopies./*Richard Wilson*

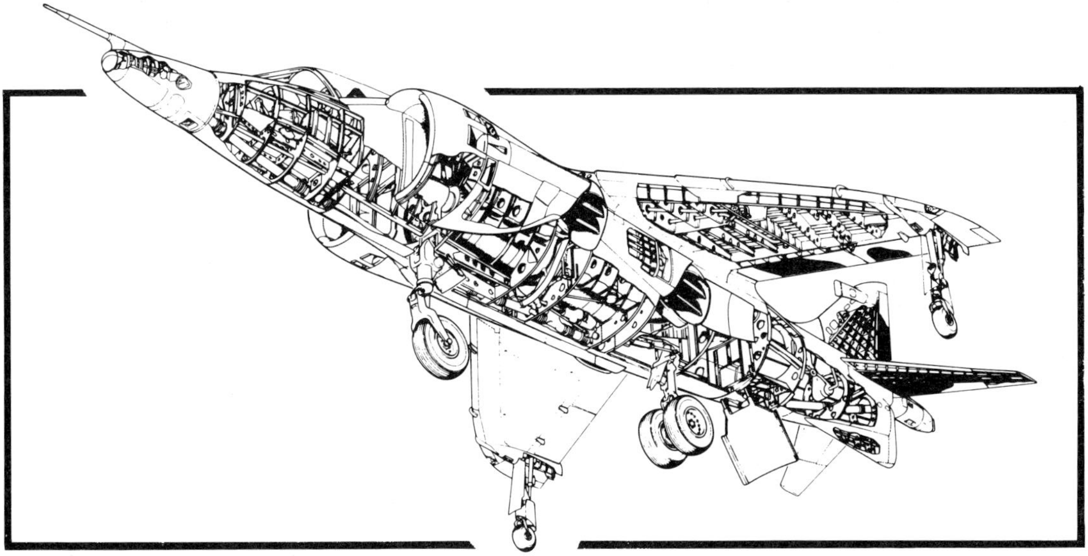

media were briefed on the programme, learning of the centreline recon pod, forthcoming uprating of the Pegasus, successful trials with air-dropped stores and dry contacts with Victors, and – from chief military executive Bob Lickley – the unit price 'in the band £750,000 to £1million, depending on quantity and equipment'. The immediate engine uprating was to 20,500lb in the Pegasus 10, achieved by better cooling of the HP turbine blades and improved water injection and combustion-chamber cooling. Other modifications included addition of a P_3 (HP delivery pressure) limiter and increased-capacity fuel pump. This engine went into production in 1969 as the Mk 102, and when retrofitted into the RAF aircraft (it was initial equipment on the AV-8A) the mark number became GR.1A. At this time the Pegasus PSP (product support programme) was funded solely by Britain, and the TBO (time between overhauls) was 200 hours, no mean figure for entry to service of so specialised a powerplant.

In 1968-9 development was centred chiefly on the nav/attack system and clearance of gunnery and weapons release. Systems of a mechanical nature, such as flight controls and hydraulics, were already superior to those of almost all previous RAF aircraft. Right from the first P.1127 a ram-air turbine (RAT) had been installed in the upper rear fuselage, extended upwards at speeds above 160 knots to provide emergency hydraulic power. It is not used after engine failure but following any failure of the engine-driven pump. With the engine out the Harrier is a poor glider (about 1:3 glide ratio) and the drill is to eject.

Obviously everything possible is done to keep the engine running, and basic reliability of the Pegasus is good for any engine, quite apart from one used for V/STOL. The main problem is birdstrikes, which are especially frequent in RAF-style missions at high speed on the deck. The engine is, of course, designed to withstand any normal birdstrike; the difficulty is aerodynamic, in that the breakup of the bird causes such flow disturbance that the engine surges. Flow becomes violently unstable, and it is common for the engine to flameout (the combustion flame goes out, leaving the engine full of fuel vapour). By 1972 a leaf had been taken from the American book in fitting a manual fuel control (MFC) system. Since then the drill with the retrofitted engines has been: birdstrike, surge, shut off fuel for 0.5 second, advance the throttle and relight, which is better than ejection.

Further development of the engine at the start of its service career eliminated surge at high altitudes by an auto-limiter on pressure ratio, while wing AOA (angle of attack) is limited to 18°. This limit is no problem, and as noted later combat manoeuvrability is today immensely augmented by viffing. Another feature of the RAF Harrier is bolt-on ferry wingtips, which by increasing span reduce induced drag and extend range. In 1977 a ferry tip of carbon fibre composite was tested to unfactored limits, at the time the largest primary structure in this material flown in Europe.

Harriers joined the RAF in January 1969 when the Harrier Conversion Unit formed at Dunsfold. After pilot conversion, the RAF became the first air service in the world to have a true off-base capability with jet combat aircraft on its 51st birthday, on 1 April 1969, when the HCU became No 233 Operational Conversion Unit at Wittering (then in Northants, now in Cambridgeshire). This unit has ever since trained Harrier pilots, for the front-line force of five squadrons. Again appropriately, the first of the latter was No 1 (motto *In omnibus princeps,* 'in all things first') which flew its Hunters to Wittering and began converting in July 1969. Next came No 4, to be based at RAF Wildenrath, Germany, followed by No 20 and No 3, forming a complete wing at the major base on the German/Dutch frontier. This wing was declared operational on 1 January 1972.

At this time an observer might have wondered why, having at last got an aircraft that could live literally at the front line, hiding in any convenient or contrived place, the Harrier squadrons should have been kept so far from any possible action. Things were partially rectified in 1977 when No 20 Squadron re-equipped with Jaguars and gave its Harriers to Nos 3 and 4 (bringing these up the the standard NATO establishment of 18 aircraft) which then moved eastwards to RAF Gutersloh less than 75 miles from East Germany and the most easterly of all Allied airfields in Germany.

These two squadrons, 3 and 4, comprise essentially the whole of RAF Germany's survivable tactical airpower, unless one believes that in the event of war an enemy would overlook the need to destroy airbases. They are supported by No 1 Sqn in the UK, which forms part of the ACE (Allied Command Europe) Mobile Force, or AMF, which is intended to redeploy in emergency to advanced bases. Likewise, in emergency, 233 OCU would stop training and deploy its aircraft in combat roles, probably to reinforce Nos 3 and 4 Squadrons.

Though Western training seldom approaches the realism and toughness of Warsaw Pact exercises, the RAF has paid more than lip-service to the vital need to become absolutely proficient in dispersed operations of the kind which would be the only ones possible in the event of any European conflict. From 1969 thousands of possible operating locations for Harriers have been surveyed – a considerable number are in the UK, though these could be of value only after the Continent had been overrun – and in an emergency an air commander would have many from which to choose. Virtually all Harrier operations, ashore or afloat, are of the STOVL (short take-off, vertical landing) type, giving the greatest weapon load and maximum sortie time and radius. Ideally a dispersed base needs as much as 400m (1,300ft) of possible take-off run, and in the author's view existing strips such as highways of adequate width are preferable to strips in virgin landscape. Some dozens of tons of hardware are needed to establish a forward dispersed base. Though well-drained grass can be used for a while, most sites would be paved with wire mesh, PSP (pierced-steel planking) or, best of all, lightweight MEXE (Military Engineering Experimental Establishment, now the MVEE at Chobham) strip specially tailored to do the job. An obvious further improvement would be the provision of quickly erected airportable ski jumps of the kind discussed in the Sea Harrier chapter. In addition, each site needs tents, chairs, tables, beds, crash

Above: Harriers of No 4 Sqn seen in a camouflaged hide on a deployment in West Germany, June 1976./*MoD*

Right: A formation of Harrier GR.3s of No 4 Squadron sweeps past a lake in West Germany during a sortie from RAF Gütersloh. /*Barry Ellson – Royal Air Force Germany/PR*

Below: Rearming a No 4 Sqn Harrier in a camouflaged dispersal in Germany. In the foreground can be seen two empty SNEB rocket pods./*Rolls-Royce*.

med
flyvekontrollen
tilladelse

Above: Tidy echelon by GR.3s of No 1 Sqn, with aircraft number in red above fin stripes./*BAe*

Above left: The aerodynamics of a rolling vertical landing become apparent in wet conditions; airspeed will be 20 to 30 knots./*BAe*

Left: Two GR.1s of No 1 Sqn (XV757 in foreground) practise hovering during the unit's first deployment to Cyprus in 1970./*BAe*

Bottom left: Harrier of No 1 Sqn. arriving at Flyvestation Vandel, the RDAF base at Jutland which was activated for the Taceval./*MoD*

Overleaf, top left: An historic Harrier – the first production standard single-seater, XV738, subsequently modified to GR.3 standard and equipped with a laser rangefinder nose, seen here in service with No 3 Squadron salvoing four SNEB rocket pods at a target range in Sardinia./*BAe*

Overleaf, bottom left: Dispersed-site operations by No 3 Squadron, showing a GR.3 with nosewheel chocked under camouflage netting (which is a lot better than nothing but a forest canopy is better). It is possible to taxi under such netting, using three narrow strips of pierced-steel planking./*BAe*

Overleaf, right: Two Harrier GR.3s of No 233 OCU, RAF Wittering, going round a loop./*Richard Wilson*

vehicles, electric generators and large amounts of maintenance gear which must include provisions for looking after flying clothing and safety equipment. Full maintenance is centred at a Squadron Maintenance Area (SMA) at or adjacent to a fixed-wing airhead. To mount a typical week-long exercise in the AMF in 1972 took from 10 to 30 loads by a C-130, but today this upper figure can be improved upon. German squadrons travel by road, of course. One could fill several books this size with interesting descriptions of dispersed-site techniques, which have been brought to a fine art in an effort to operate round the clock and, as far as possible, evade detection even by modern multi-sensor aircraft.

Life at the Hessian Hilton is not unpleasant – a lot better than being nuked, surely – and after a decade of experience always yields serviceability rates better than on fixed-base airfields. The Harrier seldom needs more than 10 MMH/FH (maintenance man-hours per flight hour), and on occasion has got it down to six or seven. As examples of what has been achieved, in the 1974 Big Tee (Tee, tactical evaluation exercise) 12 Harriers flew 364 sorties in a three-day war, an average of ten sorties per aircraft per day. They delivered the equivalent of 550 long tons of ordnance and 77,000 rounds of 30mm ammunition. And in the 1977 TEE conducted by AAFCE (Allied Air Forces Central Europe), in which operations were conducted under simulated NBC (nuclear, biological, chemical) attack, Nos 3 and 4 Sqns gained the maximum possible marks.

NBC exercises are no joke, and in any case ten sorties per aircraft per day cannot be sustained unless personnel and aircraft are very fit indeed. Pilots board via a wheeled ladder (though it always seemed possible to walk up the wing from the tip and thus make this bulky item superfluous). The inertial platform can be rapidly aligned, and within a minute of climbing aboard a pilot can be ready to take off, the engine being started by a Lucas gas turbine which also serves as an APU (auxiliary power unit) for ground power. For takeoff, the aircraft is lined up with the brakes on and the ASI (airspeed indicator) bug set to the pre-computed liftoff speed. The nozzle angle stop is set to 50° and the engine speed to 55 per cent rpm; then, brakes off and slam open the throttle, with the left hand firmly holding the nozzle lever. As the ASI needle goes past the bug the nozzle lever is pulled smartly back to the stop. The Harrier jumps into the sky, gear is retracted, and when clear of ground effect the accelerating transition takes place into wingborne flight at about 180 knots. Ground run is never as much

500th
Ski-Jump

as 1,200 feet, and at the 2,000-foot marker the Harrier should be well into its transition.

Vertical landings are the ideal, but at a dispersed site an RVL (rolling vertical landing) is usually preferred, touching down at 40 or 50 knots, to minimise reingestion and FOD (foreign-object damage). Standard drill for a landing, following normal reduction of height and forward speed, compliance with ATC procedures, and completion of routine landing checks (the latter including putting on full flap at the same time gear is selected), begins with selection of 20° nozzle on the downwind leg at a normal height of 500ft. This provides power for the RCVs, and the RCV pressure gauge is given a glance. Lined up with the landing direction, 40° nozzle is selected and the aircraft positioned about 3,000ft (1,000m) short of the landing spot; the chief instrument used is called the ADD (airstream direction detector) or the AOA (angle of attack indicator), and it is held at 8° to 9° solely by the stick. The aim is to arrive 3,000ft from the landing spot at 50 feet, where the nozzle lever is pulled back to Hover Stop. Cracking the nozzles gives mild nose-up trim.

From this 50ft point there are two choices available for a landing. In the vertical landing (VL) all the pilot need do is momentarily reduce rpm very slightly (the book says 1–2%) in order to set up a selected rate of descent. The pilot looks ahead and senses the surrounding horizon, keeping attitude and position correct with stick and rudder. The moment the wheels hit, the throttle is shut to Idle, nozzles switched aft and the parking brake applied. The alternative is the rolling vertical landing (RVL). Preferred whenever any form of ingestion could be a problem, this involves switching the nozzle lever forward from Hover Stop to the 80° position, without reducing rpm. This both sets up the required positive rate of descent and at the same time accelerates the aircraft forward, so that the wheels touch at about 40 knots. Immediately the throttle is chopped and brakes applied, as before.

To an experienced fighter or attack pilot the Harrier is no problem, and it opens new vistas for personal skills and offers new excitement each time the left hand goes to the throttle and nozzle lever. Most ex-helicopter pilots have initially found it a real struggle to stay mentally up with, or ahead of, the Harrier; and being even a little behind can be dangerous. The task of converting pilots is thus more than usually important, and most observers would take it for granted it needs a dual two-seat aircraft. But because of the ludicrous British political environment at the start of the programme a dual

Above left: Hovering GR.3 of No 4 Sqn. RAF Germany, showing the EMI five-camera centreline pod often carried by this unit./*BAe*

Left: A 1979 photograph recording the 500th ski jump, by a GR.3 (XZ136) with BL.755 bomblet dispensers./*BAe*

Below left: Though a major job, engine changes are possible during dispersed field operations; aircraft letter Y in yellow, probably No. 3 Sqn./*BAe*

Below: The first T.2 prototype, pictured during fin development and with anti-spin parachute fitted. Pressurised volume rose in this version from 41 to 85 cubic feet./*BAe*

Overleaf, left: Harrier GR.3 of No 1 Squadron returns to RAF Wittering after a squadron exchange visit to Italy – note the large ferry tanks on the inboard wing pylons./*Martin Horseman*

Overleaf, top right: Superb portrait of a GR.3 of No 233 OCU, with aircraft letter on tail in pale blue./*BAe*

Overleaf, bottom right: US Marine Corps AV-8A Harrier of VMA-231 aboard USS *Franklin D. Roosevelt* during the squadron's deployment with the carrier's Air Group in 1977./*Gordon Bain*

L

NM
2225
NAVY
112
0639
406NM
104
406
NM
VA-215
500NM
NM
500
607

P.1127 – though studied in the same week the 1127 first ran its engine, in September 1960 – was a total non-starter. Five years were to pass before Hawker project engineers picked up the work again, and then in 1965 a full feasibility study was begun on a dual P.1127RAF. Not until 1967 was cover obtained for two development aircraft (XW174-5) the first of which eventually flew on 24 April 1969.

Even then much had to be done to develop a production Harrier T.2, and it was not until August 1970 that the first was accepted at 233 OCU at Wittering. By this time most of the basic conversion of the pilots for the RAF Harrier force had been completed.

The Air Staff Requirement that was eventually written called for the T.2 to be used as a dual type-conversion trainer and also as a vehicle to speed proficiency in the Harrier nav/attack system, though as this system is used only in conventional flight the task could have been done with a fixed-wing machine such as a Hunter. The primary task was training in V/STOL techniques, and the further important proviso was made that the T.2 should be able to fly Harrier combat missions and form part of the RAF combat inventory. With the rear seat and tail ballast removed the T.2 came out about 800lb heavier than

Top left: Harrier GR.3 from No 233 OCU based at RAF Wittering flying over the mountains of northern Scotland./*MoD*

Centre left: Harrier GR.3s of No 3 Sqn during Exercise 'Oak Stroll'. / *MoD*

Bottom left: Company two-seater G-VTOL making a slow (about 90 knots) landing at Dunsfold after heavy rain./*BAe*

Above: A No 1 Sqn Harrier GR.3 hooks onto a Victor K.2 of No 57 Sqn during an air refuelling exercise./*MoD*

Overleaf, top left: A fine study of the second YAV-8B in cruising mode with Snakeye bombs and Sidewinders./*MCAir*

Overleaf, bottom left: Line maintenance on a VA-1 Matador of Essa 008 at Rota./*Rolls-Royce*

Overleaf, top right: The Sea Harrier of Lt-Cdr T. J. H. Gedge, CO of No 800 Squadron, with Sidewinders and a touch of flap./*BAe*

Overleaf, bottom right: Sea Harriers of No 700A (now 899) Squadron, Royal Navy, aboard HMS *Hermes* in 1979./*BAe*

158395
2

008
4

ROYAL NAVY
250
N

50
100
101

the Harrier GR.1 (today the margin is nearer 700lb), but it was given the same weapon carriage provisions. In the training role the two-seater is some 1,400lb heavier in the equipped empty condition.

Heading the list of development tasks was maintaining weathercock (yaw) stability and the correct relationship between cg and both the wing aerodynamic centre and the engine thrust centre in the jet-lift mode. Modifying the forward fuselage was straightforward: the nose was moved forward 47 inches, the inclined seat frame (now the rear seat frame) moved 7 inches to the rear, the cabin-conditioning system enlarged and repackaged immediately behind the large tandem canopies hinged on the right, the nose RCV moved forward near the very tip of the nose, and the inertial platform and F.95 camera relocated under the rear seat. The stepped tandem seating imposes no significant increase in drag, and gives the instructor a better all-round view than that of the pilot of a single-seater, including 10° below the horizon directly ahead. Even the front-seater has a rearward view better than in the single-seat Harrier, while his forward view is unchanged.

To balance the destabilising effect of the new front end the T.2 tail was moved 33.3 inches to the rear and raised 11 inches on a new fixed structure above the existing rear fuselage. The tailcone was greatly extended and (for development flying) fitted with a

Above left: Pegasus engine being refitted in a No 233 OCU Harrier trainer at RAF Wittering./*Rolls-Royce*

Below left: A brochure-type presentation picture of the Harrier and some representative (and some not so representative, eg the SRAAM AAMs) stores which were to be carried by aircraft in RAF service./*BAe Kingston*

Above: Harrier GR.3 of No 4 Sqn during Exercise 'Heath Fir' in West Germany./*Crown Copyright*

Below: Lineup of Harrier GR.3s from RAF Germany squadrons at a tactical fighter meet in May 1978 at RAF Leuchars, Scotland./*MoD*

Above: XW175 development two-seater making vertical landing at Dunsfold with original short fin in 1970./*BAe*

Below: XW264 was the first production T.2, pictured at Dunsfold. /*BAe*

Left: Sea Harrier FRS.1 of No 801 Naval Air Squadron landing on HMS *Invincible,* 1 June 1981./*Denis Calvert*

brake/anti-spin parachute as well as a rear RCV much further aft. The underfin was changed in shape and enlarged, and the equipment-cooling ram-air inlet built into the front of the added fin-base structure. With the pitch and yaw RCVs moved right to the extremeties of the longer nose and tail it was confirmed that V/STOL control was little different from a GR.1, with only a modest increase in bleed-air consumption. At high wing angles of attack, however, weathercock stability was inadequate, and at first this was attributed to the wake from the raised canopies. Removal of the cabin air scoops just behind the rear canopy made no difference, and the next step was to raise the height of the fin, at first by 6 inches. This did little, so the top of the fin was given an 18-inch extension, with a kinked leading edge. This resulted in a marked improvement, but further extension was most unwelcome because the increased stresses would have demanded redesign of the rear fuselage, with penalties in commonality and structure weight. A 23-inch extension was flown, however, at strictly limited airspeeds and sideslip angles, and the result was excellent. After much further work an ideal answer was found in a broader-chord and better engineered 18-inch extension, together with automatic extension of the airbrake to 26° whenever the tailplane was driven to a really high angle of attack.

This new fin was actually a retrofit on early T.2s, because production had not been held up during the search for a good minimum-change solution to the weathercock problem. The only other tail modification was to add shotfilled tubes at the tips of

the tailplane to damp out ground-running buzz caused by the fact that the longer T.2 fuselage has a natural frequency that is a sub-harmonic of that of the tailplane. Thus, while T.2 tailplanes can fly on any Harrier, no two-seater is permitted to fly with a single-seat tailplane.

Though the first production T.2 (XW264) was delivered in July 1970, it was another 13 months before the definitive tail made its appearance at 233 OCU. Subsequently each of the operational squadrons has had a two-seater, used for Instrument Ratings, weapon-delivery instruction and various other forms of checks and tests, as well as forming part of the combat inventory. The US Marine Corps TAV-8A is covered in the next chapter. Mention must also be made of British Aerospace's very useful civil Mk 52 demonstrator registered G-VTOL, assembled from parts contributed by all suppliers on an embodiment-loan basis to provide a go-anywhere demonstrator equipped with full Airways navaids including ADF and ILS. First flown on 16 September 1971, G-VTOL was the first two-seater with the Pegasus 102, earlier examples still having the Mk 101 at that time.

By early 1972 G/VTOL was being retrofitted with a still more powerful Pegasus, which today is still the standard in-service engine. Designated Pegasus 11, Mk 103, it introduced a rebladed fan (both rotors and stators) to increase mass flow. This increase thrust from all four nozzles, and is augmented by improved HP turbine cooling, permitting an increase in entry temperature from 1,486°K (2,215°F) to 1,511°K (2,260°F). Further improvements include revision to the combustion chamber and the manual fuel control system. The Mk 103 engine was type-tested in February 1971 and approved five months later. When fitted to a Harrier GR.1A the aircraft mark number was changed to GR.3; likewise the T.2 re-engined with the Pegasus 103 became the T.4. A listing of numbers of each mark of Harrier appears in the Appendices.

Since entry to service the increase in engine power has been accompanied by numerous engineering modifications, almost all of a routine nature, such as the gradual introduction of the much better 12kVA alternator (as on the AV-8A) instead of two of the old 4kVA machines, and the Mk 2 Lucas gas-turbine starter/APU with electrical output raised from 1½ to 6kVA. Part of the electric uprating was to handle two major additions which improve combat capability and also change external appearance. The first of the new equipments was a laser ranger and marked-target seeker (LRMTS). The model selected, and in fact developed for this application and in related form for the Jaguar, is the Ferranti Type 106. This comprises an active laser and a receiver, together with

Above: G-VTOL making a ski launch at 15°; at this angle end-speeds as low as 42 knots were recorded. Studies have been made of road-portable ski-jumps./*Rolls-Royce*

Right: Three-view of Harrier T.2/T.4./*BAe*

Below: Harrier of No 20 Sqn hovering during Exercise 'Grimm Charade' in West Germany./*MoD*

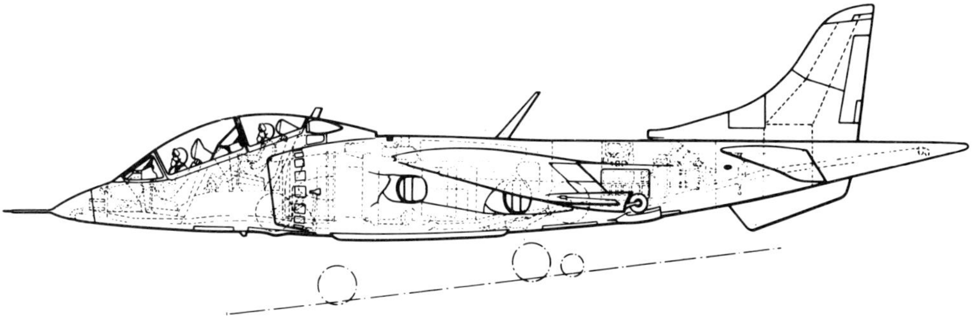

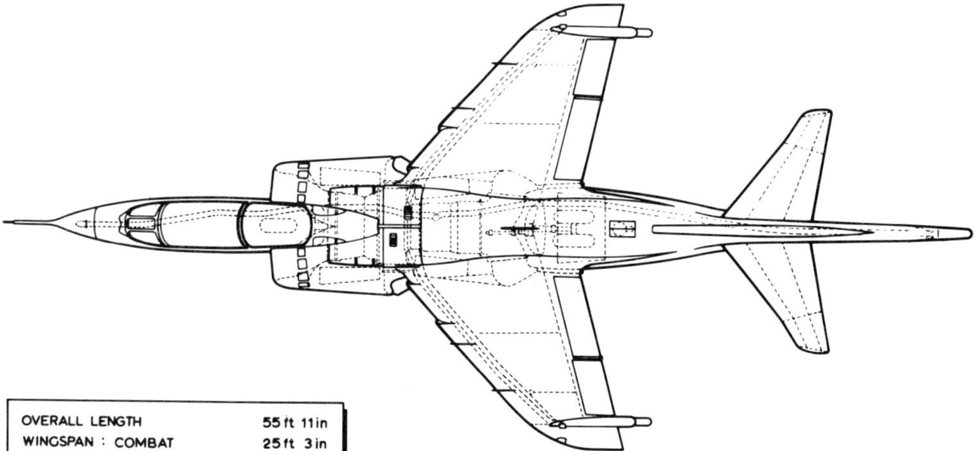

OVERALL LENGTH	55 ft 11 in
WINGSPAN : COMBAT	25 ft 3 in
FERRY	29 ft 8 in
HEIGHT (GROUND ATTITUDE)	13 ft 8 in

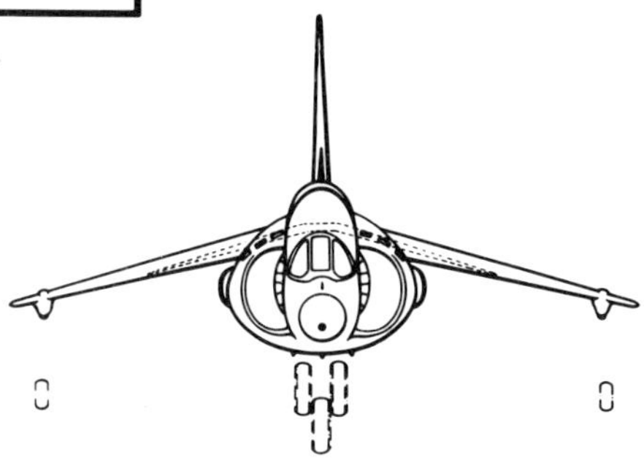

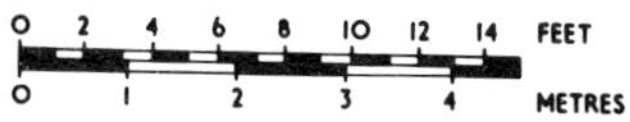

Above: The first LRMTS-equipped Harrier T. 4 for the RAF seen at Dunsfold, 24 February 1976./*BAe Kingston*

Right: RAF maintenance team towing a Harrier out of an inflatable hide at dispersal in Belize./*MoD*

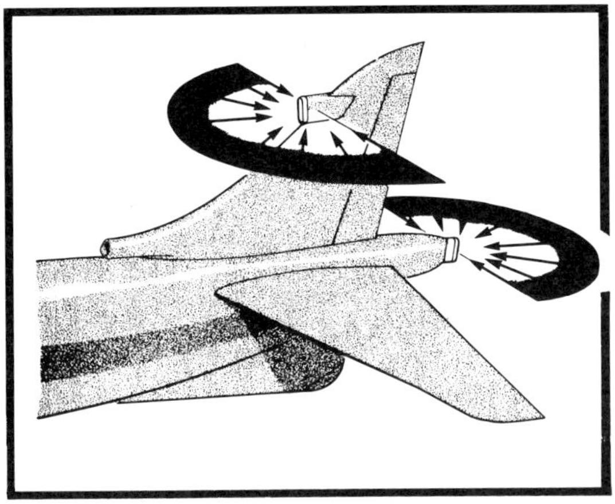

Left: Together the front and rear passive aerials of the RWR give all-round coverage./*BAe*

Below: Harrier of No 1 Sqn, usually based at RAF Wittering, seen on the ground in Belize in November 1975./*MoD*

electronics and a data interface to tie it in with the rest of the nav/attack system. The laser is a typical compact Nd-YAG type, stabilized 360° in roll and ±25° in pitch, and emits pulses of laser light at from 2 to 10 or more pulses per second, on pilot command. Under all attack conditions it can be directed ahead or within a 20° cone, if necessary under command from the nav/attack system, and is space-stabilized to ensure accurate pointing at the desired target. In this mode it sends back continuous and precise data on target range, range rate (speed of closure) and angles, normally presented on the HUD. In the marked-target mode the laser is not initially used; the ground target is identified and marked by a laser carried by friendly troops. The Harrier LRMTS seeker searches automatically and instantly detects any marked target. Finding one, it locks-on and ranges, presenting its position, plus the other information, on the pilot's HUD.

The LRMTS was tested in a Ferranti Canberra in 1970, flown in various Harriers and fitted as initial equipment to XZ128, the first of the final GR.3 batch (and the 207th Harrier built) in 1976. By this time several squadron aircraft had been retrofitted, and all GR.3 Harriers had the LRMTS by 1979. It has no effect on flight performance or handling.

The other addition was an RWR, radar warning receiver. As a diagram shows, this comprises two passive aerials, one facing forward from near the top of the fin and the other facing to the rear from the extremity of the tailcone downstream of the rear RCVs. The system is the ARI.18223, by MSDS (Marconi Space and Defence Systems), and is a single-seat version of the generally similar 18228 whose display CRT (cathode-ray tube) faces the navigator in RAF Phantoms and Buccaneers. Obviously the Harrier installation provides a display for the pilot, together with an attention-getter. The purpose of the RWR is to inform the pilot if any hostile radiation is illuminating the aircraft (from enemy radars, for example), and possibly its type, signal strength and direction. These data are processed in such a way as to minimise the extra pilot workload and assist him in deciding on the best course of action. Obviously tactical aircraft need defensive systems such as jammers and dispensed chaff, jammers or flare payloads, but the Harrier has had no such protection, and hastily contrived lash-ups were fitted in the Falklands, as described later. Today there is at last funding for a comprehensive ECM suite, the Zeus. This will be produced by Marconi and Northrop, and installed by BAe.

6 The Marines' AV-8A

In the jet V/STOL heyday of the early 1960s it had been taken for granted that the world's military air arms would deploy V/STOL jets in very large numbers before the end of that decade. With the collapse of NBMR-3 and cancellation of the P.1154 the whole idea virtually fizzled out, except in the Soviet Union where its importance had been recognised. France stopped the Mirage IIIV, and all that was left by the late 1960s was the subsonic Harrier in which few foreign countries showed more than passing interest. Hawker Siddeley mounted a low-key campaign to try to educate air forces in the future technique of V/STOL tactical operations, both ashore and afloat, but its overt attempts to sell the Harrier itself were directed at a small range of nations. It was thus quite unexpected when a commissionaire guarding the Hawker Siddeley chalet at the 1968 SBAC show at Farnborough announced the arrival of three officers from the US Marine Corps who said they were interested in flying the Harrier.

They had not suddenly become interested from watching the company pilots perform at the show. The Marines had been the greatest early pioneers of V/STOL warfare when from 1949 they had refined what became the technique of 'vertical envelopment' in which helicopters based on assault ships invade a hostile beach and, having established a beach-head, keep it resupplied. The snag, of course, was that the assault force had to provide firepower to protect the helicopters, and though opposition was generally light in Korea it was recognised that in other conflicts enemy fighters and anti-aircraft fire might shoot down all the helicopters before a bridgehead could be secured. Jet V/STOL appeared to be the only answer, and the Marine Corps kept a close watch on this field. But by 1967 the only actual hardware available for aerial firepower over the beach-head was another helicopter, the Army-developed Lockheed AH-56A Cheyenne. This impressive and extremely costly machine was packed with electronics but was diametrically opposed to Marine philosophies.

Two of the better-known names for a Marine are a Grunt and a Leatherneck. They describe a tough fighting-man who needs simple and reliable equipment. The AH-56A was anything but; the Army was unhappy with both the product and the price, and eventually it was terminated in 1969. The only alternative was CTOL (conventional takeoff and landing) airpower, in the shape of the Marines' A-4s and F-4s. But these had to be conveyed in a giant Fleet Carrier and either based aboard this ship or on a purpose-constructed airfield at the beach-head. Many millions were spent developing the SATS (short airfield for tactical support), which meant filling ships with aluminium planking, gas-turbine catapults, arrester wires and much other gear, as well as a complete 'Seabee' Construction Battalion for about two weeks (if the enemy did not interfere) fixing everything together.

Ideally the situation cried out for a jet V/STOL, and the Marines were desperate to see an effective one developed. Even if it played no offensive role, such an aircraft was judged capable of gaining air superiority over the beach-head and of protecting the helicopters. Marines had never flown with the TES Kestrels, but one or two officers had subsequently flown the same aircraft as XV-6As at Edwards and talked with NASA at Langley, where there were two more, about future possibilities. There were many half-baked schemes for American jet V/STOL combat aircraft, including a Navy study for a Fighter/Attack Technology Prototype (this led to the XFV-12A, discussed in the penultimate chapter). For the foreseeable future there was in 1968 no jet V/STOL in sight except the Harrier, and what the Marine Corps wanted to know was: could it do a useful job?

Long before this the news that the Marines were looking at the Harrier was causing ripples through the Pentagon. The Air Force and Navy were openly sceptical of V/STOL in general and the little British jet in particular. Neither had any plans to buy the British aircraft, but it was something the United States did not have, and in January 1969 both services had full evaluation teams at Dunsfold and Boscombe. Tragically, one of the Air Force team, Maj Charles R. Rosberg, was killed in the first fatal accident in the entire Hawker jet V/STOL programme. Despite this

Above right: February 1971, and an AV-8A from Pax River is spotted on the deck of LPH-7 *Guadalcanal* during early trials at sea./*USN*

Right: A few weeks later another AV-8A was making free takeoffs from the same ship with FR probe installed. Note the USMC badge. /*USN*

MARINES

Left: The first wet hook up with a 'buddy' A-4M was made by an aircraft of VMA-513 on 3 March 1971./*USN*

Centre left: Positioning a Snakeye bomb under the left inboard pylon of a VMA-513 aircraft aboard *Guadalcanal* on 22 March 1971./*USN*

Centre right: June 1973 and an AV-8A of VMA-542 makes a vertical ascent from LPD-1 *Raleigh* during Project Battle Cry./*USN*

Bottom left: Sqn Ldr Tom Lecky-Thompson takes off from a disused coal yard near St Pancras station, London, in the fourth production Harrier GR.1, XV741, at the start of his westbound winning flight during the *Daily Mail* trans-Atlantic Air Race in May 1969. The Harrier's time of 5hr 57min and its arrival in the centre of New York City made a major impression in the US at the time when the US Marine Corps order was under consideration, in Congress.

the reports of both teams were highly positive, parts of the USAF evaluation being almost lyrical in nature, and later this did much to spread the true gospel through the US defence machine. The Navy evaluation was particularly important because all Marine Corps aircraft are procured by the Navy, though on a separate financial vote. But the ripples persisted, and gathered strength. They revolved around two parrot-cries, whose meanings were sufficiently obscure for them to be hard to nail.

One parrot-cry was that the Harrier was 'a foreign airplane'. It is extremely unusual for the United States to import any aircraft, military or civil, and when it does the giant US planemaking industry and its Congressmen lose no time in making angry speeches. Clearly, whereas other nations in Europe, Asia, Australia and many other places buy military aircraft *because* they are American, when the reverse happens the fur begins to fly. And the campaign against this foreign product was initially founded upon the supposed fact that it was pretty useless. Even a former British Air Minister, Hugh Fraser, had helpfully told the Commons that the Harrier 'from a military point of view is a toy, unable to carry any weapons, unable to have a great range, and unable to fly above sonic speed'. All four statements were factually incorrect, but the media love controversy and rebuttals get about 1% of the coverage of the original statement. In the United States a popular interpretation of this criticism, syndicated from Coast to Coast, was 'The Harrier couldn't carry a box of matches across a football field'.

Against all this barricade of nonsense was a band of fighting-men, keenly aware of the need for political muscle on Capitol Hill and tireless in their search for ways to do a better job. Masterminding the search for tactical airpower without an airfield was Gen G. McCutcheon, USMC. The team he sent to the Farnborough airshow in 1968 was headed by Brig-Gen Johnson and included two test pilots, Col Tom Miller and Lt-Col Bud Baker. Their evaluation of the Harrier was complete and highly favourable. Contrary to the widespread American belief, it could fly useful combat missions, had plenty of range, and promised still more when re-engined with the Pegasus 11. Contract negotiations began within two weeks, and the Marine Corps decided even at this early date not just to buy a trial batch but to go all-out for V/STOL with a total procurement of 114 aircraft. This had previously been calculated to be adequate to support a force of four 20-aircraft squadrons, the rest serving for training and attrition. Money previously earmarked for F-4J Phantoms was taken from the FY70 (Fiscal Year 1970, starting on 1 July 1969) budget and allocated to a first batch of 12 aircraft, designated AV-8A in the US system in which V indicates an aircraft with V/STOL capability and the prefix A indicates Attack.

As far as possible the AV-8A was made identical with the Harrier GR.1, though it changed with the years. Subsequent buys included 18 with FY71 funds, 30 with FY72 and 30 with FY73, bringing the total to 90. By this time the Marines felt it was politically safe to buy the two-seater, for initial conversion to the AV-8A and for continuation training at squadron level as in the RAF. The extra cost of these reduced the final batch from 24 to 20, made up of 12 AV-8As and eight two-seaters designated TAV-8A. From the start of US interest it had been appreciated that political obstacles would largely disappear if the Harrier could be manufactured in the United States. This was not possible for the initial 12 AV-8As, but the possibility of licence-production of the remaining aircraft was exhaustively examined and a licence worked out with McDonnell Douglas at St Louis. In October 1971 a further licence was signed between Rolls-Royce (1971) Ltd and Pratt & Whitney Aircraft for joint further development of the Pegasus engine (designated F402 in the United States) and possible licence production by the American company. For both the airframe and engine it was concluded that the quantities and rates of production were too small to bear the increased costs of licence manufacture, but joint collaboration between the four companies has continued.

The major new feature of the AV-8A, which went into production in 1970, was the Pegasus 11, which did not reach the RAF as a retrofit until two years later. Even so, the first ten AV-8As were initially delivered with the Pegasus 10, designated Mk 802 for export and in the USMC called F402-RR-400. These first ten aircraft also lacked an emergency fuel control (later retrofitted) which in the usual American

manner provides direct manual throttle control as a back-up, as explained earlier. This manual provision was later also adopted by the RAF, becoming an integral fitment with the Mk 103 engine. The RAF also later adopted several other changes requested by the USMC for the AV-8A.

Most of the changes required resulted from the different spectrum of American weapons and missions. Whereas the prime RAF Harrier mission has always been first-pass low-level attack on a fixed surface target, that of the USMC has been a versatile capability for multiple dive attacks on land or sea targets in visual conditions, with a strong secondary need for air combat. This put the emphasis on air-to-air weapons, whilst making the complex and costly FE.541 nav/attack system look less attractive to a service whose 'troops are warriors rather than mechanics'. The inertial system was, in fact, accepted as part of the original fit, but in 1972-74 it was removed from the AV-8A force in the apparent belief that the Marines only go to war when the weather is good. Another item carefully studied was the gun; at first it was intended to return the Aden packages to Britain as soon as an American equivalent could be cleared for service, but the British gun soon established such a good reputation that it remains to this day, even though it cannot fire standard US 30mm ammunition.

One of the few new original-equipment changes in the AV-8A was wiring for two Sidewinder air-to-air missiles on the outboard pylons; this simple missile could easily be carried by any Harrier. There is no radar so the IR-homing head cannot be slaved to its targets, but results of independent IR scanning have been adequate even with the AIM-9E Sidewinder fitted originally. Today the much better AIM-9J or -9L are becoming more common. In the 1970 AV-8A specification there were numerous minor changes in materials, radios and systems, notably removal of FE.541 and installation of a Smiths HUD and weapon-aiming computer (together abbreviated as Hudwac), with selectable modes such as CCIP (continuously computed impact point) symbology for air/surface weapon delivery. Another retrofit in service was to replace the Mk 9D seat by the American Stencel SIII-S3.

Delivery of the first AV-8A took place at Dunsfold on 20 November 1970, followed by a further ceremony at the US Naval Air Test Center (NATC) at Patuxent River (commonly called Pax River), in Maryland close to Washington DC. Pax River handles the BIS (Board of Inspection and Survey) trials of all new Navy and Marines aircraft, and the first four AV-8As passed BIS with flying colours by March 1971. In the course of these trials the performance envelope was examined very fully, including at least one situation not previously attempted. This was because of the inquiring nature of the Marine Corps AV-8A Project Officer, Maj Harry W. Blot. He flew the first AV-8A to arrive at Pax River and soon decided that, while it had an excellent thrust/weight ratio, superb handling and an engine that kept running even in the most adverse inlet conditions, it could not be considered as a promising fighter. Pilot view to the rear was poor, and because of the extremely small wing it was impossible to pull many g in tight manoeuvres except right at the upper end of the speed envelope. The one unexplored factor was viffing (VIFF = vectoring in forward flight). By suddenly swivelling the nozzles there seemed to be the possibility of applying extra upward or even rearward forces that might provide a new dimension in air combat.

Blot was under the mistaken impression that viffing was common practice in RAF Harrier squadrons – though bold RAF spirits had indeed played with it.

Above, far left: Air-to-ground attack with monster Zuni rockets by an AV-8A of VMA-542 in September 1974./*BAe*

Above left: 10 November 1976 and a sortie is imminent by an aircraft of VMA-231, still chained to CV-42 *Franklin D Roosevelt* in the Mediterranean./*USN*

Above: In USMC operation takeoffs are often vertical; this was by VMA-231 from the *FDR* during the Mediterranean deployment. /*USN*

Above right: Aircraft of VMA-513 aboard LPH-3 *Guam* with pilot on cockpit checks./*USN*

Below: The AV-8C is the result of the most cost effective improvement programme that could reasonably be devised for the existing AV-8A force in 1979. Among the few items showing externally are extra avionics aerials./*MCAir*

As test sorties were at a premium, he decided to by-pass intermediate points and go straight to the full reverse thrust at 500 knots. It should also be explained that, to keep a good lookout in all directions for other traffic, he was in the habit of leaving his seat harness loose. He set himself the task of timing the deceleration from 500 to 300 knots, to see how far, in a combat situation, this could force a hostile aircraft on the AV's tail to overshoot and fly into Blot's HUD-sight. In Blot's words (written for *Rolls-Royce Magazine):* 'With pencil in hand I slammed the nozzle lever into the braking stop (reverse thrust) position. The airplane started decelerating at an alarming rate, the magnitude of which I could not determine because my nose was pressed up against the sight. A terrible way to be, even in an imagined conflict. My movements were even further constrained by the fact that the violence of the manoeuvre had dislodged me from the seat, and I was now straddling the stick with my right hand extended backwards between my legs trying to hold on for dear life'.

As the AV did not come apart, and the engine kept running, he was able to make a normal landing and think things over. Apart from deciding to compromise his strap-in procedure, Blot judged that, if the powerful new force of vectored thrust could be properly harnessed, dogfighting would indeed be revolutionised. Accordingly NASA flew a special VIFF test programme in late 1971 with an XV-6A, in the course of which this low-powered but lightweight machine was tangled against a T-38 Talon. More extensive ACM (air combat manoeuvring) trials were then flown at Point Mugu, California, by the first AV-8A unit, VMA-513, formed in April 1971 at Beaufort (pronounced Bew-fort), South Carolina, under Bud Baker. A joint US/UK programme on viffing was then run in parallel with a second ACM exercise in late 1972 by VMA-513 at China Lake, California. The considered conclusion of these trials, news of which had spread and resulted in almost every available combat type joining in, was that 'With proper use of vectored thrust there is no known tactical aircraft in the world that can remain behind the AV-8A if the latter's pilot does not desire it to do so'.

This position was reached while the viff technique was in its infancy. The US/UK test lasted ten days and was run from RAF Valley over the Aberporth missile range, and involved a first phase in which dogfights were mounted between a Harrier with a strengthened nozzle drive and special instrumentation and a normal (non-viffing) Harrier, a Hunter and a Phantom FGR.2. No matter how inferior the starting position, the viffing Harrier invariably won the engagement. Results were so startling a Phase 2 programme was run against other foes, including a Lightning F.6, and viffing was examined in attacks on surface targets to assist weapon delivery and avoidance of ground fire. Again, results were excellent, and often intriguing.

Prolonged computer simulations, initially at McDonnell's St Louis plant, threw up the discouraging news that viffing at low speeds, in which the RCV controls (called RCS, reaction-control system, by MCAir) predominate, not only could not possibly result in such rapid turn rates as pilots reported but also would inevitably result in nose-over-tail tumbling. It was Harry Blot who disproved the latter prediction. Further computer simulations – some perhaps slightly suspect – worked out various procedures for evading hostile dogfighters, notably the MiG-21, and even for flying through particular manoeuvres at low level which, should the enemy pilot be unwise enough to follow through, are guaranteed to make the enemy fly into the ground.

By the end of 1972 a large range of impressive viffing manoeuvres in level, climbing and diving flight, and including flips and square turns entirely new to air combat, had been worked out and perfected. There followed several hundred viffing missions on an instrumented range against various simulated Warsaw Pact fighters. The results were officially judged impressive, and incidentally confirmed that, thanks to the exceptionally low fuel consumption compared with other modern jets achieving a similar thrust/weight ratio, it was invariably the opposition which, despite much greater fuel capacity, had to break off the fight on the grounds of fuel state. The only nagging problems were restrictions on nozzle angles at high airspeeds and the annoying need to check engine parameters prior to inflight vectoring. Most Harrier pilots also wished they had even more thrust, to beat the modern low-wing-loading dogfighters manoeuvring in the vertical plane.

Rather unexpectedly all the restrictions vanished in 1973-74 mainly to pressure from Kingston. The first modification was a refined production version of the beefed-up nozzle system. Even more important was what was called a 'combat plug', a screw-in turbine temperature fuse that allows pilots to pull significantly more power when wingborne. The two-minute installation of the plug (said Blot) gave more extra thrust than 20 years of development of the A-4 engines. As a result, for periods not exceeding 2½ minutes – which is about the elapsed time for a typical dogfight – any number of viffing cycles, typically averaging 7 seconds each, could be made at much higher thrust, and without needing to think about the engine at all. In Blot's words: 'The plug-equipped bird did everything asked of it. The Harrier had crossed the line from being good to being great . . . its ACM capability is absolutely eye-watering!'

Much has been written elsewhere of the countless exercises flown by Marine Corps AV-8As, of their many seagoing deployments (covered briefly in the next chapter) and also of the numerous losses

suffered. In simple numbers the AV-8A attrition has been similar to that of the RAF: about 30 write-offs in ten years out of a 100-strong force. But the contrasts are astonishing. For one thing, the RAF Harriers spend almost all their time at very high speed at extremely low level, which is invariably below the minimum altitude for other air forces. The AV-8As spend their time at all altitudes up to about 35,000 feet often involving prolonged air-combat or ground-attack dive manoeuvres. Moreover, whereas the RAF suffered an unremarkable loss rate in the first six years and has since reduced it to a commendably low level, the Marine Corps did fantastically well in the first four years and then ran into a spate of accidents.

Listing RAF accidents and causes is hampered by the fact that in Britain such information is not made available to the public, in contrast to the open reporting of other Western countries. Within this limitation considerable information can still be collected. One point worth making is that in the early years with their agile jet V/STOL the Marines trod carefully and among other things picked test pilots and second-tour aviators who flew by the book and had a mature outlook. But this, according to Tom Miller (now a general), made it look as if the AV could be flown 'only by supermen. So we switched the policy and took aviators on a wider basis including some straight from flight school'. Conversion of first-tour aviators, especially before the TAV was available, led to a lot of incidents put down to pilot error, most of them at the time (typically after 30 to 100 hours) at which the pilot feels he can 'hack it' and starts to relax. But at no time has there been any evidence of particular difficulty or danger in either the V/STOL or wing-borne modes, except perhaps for need for especial concentration when crabbing in a strong cross-wind to a vertical landing (though to get into sideslip trouble a pilot has to ignore the autostab, yaw vane and rudder-pedal shaker).

By 1976 the Marines had their complete single-seat AV-8A force, which was formed into Marine Air Group 32, with home base at Cherry Point, North Carolina. Apart from the pioneer VMA-513 it includes VMA-542 and VMA-231, and the training squadron VMAT-203. The front-line squadrons have piled up immense experience operating in all kinds of missions and environments, including dedicated aircraft carriers as well as the usual sea bases of LPHs

Top: May 1979 and first flight from St Louis of the first AV-8C, rebuilt and re-equipped by MCAir using many parts from the UK. /*MCAir*

Far left: The Marines deliberately delayed ordering their two-seaters until 1975 because they were fearful of Congress cutting off funds for the main AV-8A force. Liftoff at Dunsfold of the first TAV-8A in 1976. Though assigned to VMA(T)-203 for training, they also carry special radios for control of Marine ground forces./*BAe*

Left: VA-1 of Essa 008 aboard PA-01 *Dédalo*; the wooden planks are quite unworried by jet V/STOL, though the pitch sometimes melted. /*Rolls-Royce*

(landing platform, helicopter) and LHAs (landing, helicopter assault). VMA-513 has been based at Iwakuni, Japan, and at Yuma, Arizona, while squadrons rotate on detachment to Okinawa.

Despite the widespread use in US tactical units of 'smart' (laser-guided) missiles, the AV-8A has never been retrofitted with a laser nose. By 1973 all had been retrofitted with the Mk 803 (F402-RR-402) engine, and during the period 1979-84 three-quarters of the surviving AV-8A force, or 60 aircraft, are being recycled through Cherry Point's extensive engineering workshops to emerge as completely updated aircraft designated AV-8C (as related in Chapter 8 this designation was originally to refer to a different variant). The biggest 8C task is a complete structural rework under a SLEP (service life extension program) to clear the airframe for 4,000 hours' combat flying. On top of this is a CILOP (conversion in lieu of procurement) programme which adds the AV-8B type LIDs (lift-improvement devices) to increase mission load, greatly enhanced EW (electronic warfare) equipment, an on-board oxygen generator, improved UHF communications radio and the KY-58 secure voice transmission system. Full details of the EW update are not available, but they include RWR in the tailcone, forward-looking passive warning aerials at the wingtips (instead of on the fin, as in Harriers) and a Goodyear ALE-39 dispenser in the rear equipment

bay for chaff payloads, jammers or flares. MCAir supplied the first kits for the 8C update conversions to be done at St Louis, and is continuing to supply kits to Cherry Point, with components supplied by BAe Kingston.

There is another operator of the AV-8A, though the aircraft are almost unchanged. In 1972 the Spanish government began discussions with the British government and Hawker Siddeley, as a result of which John Farley flew a Harrier out to the small 35-year-old carrier *Dédalo* and demonstrated what

the aircraft could do. To the surprise of everyone but the British, the wood-planked deck was not even scorched. This was clearly what the Spanish Arma Aérea (naval aviation) wanted; they planned to build a modern Sea Control Ship (SCS), with help from the Americans who at that time were eager to build SCSs themselves. In the event the Spanish had to buy the SCS design and get on with the ships themselves, with expert help from Gibbs and Cox of New York. By 1984 they should commission their first V/STOL carrier, at present known merely as PA-01, rather smaller than HMS *Invincible* but with a properly engineered bow ski-jump.

With the ship in hand in 1973 the Navy Minister, Admiral da Veiga y Sanz, announced a requirement for 24 Harriers. The stumbling-block was that a future Labour government in Britain was almost certain to cancel any contract, so an uncancellable deal was worked out whereby Britain sold to the US government, the aircraft were shipped to the USA and MCAir in St Louis did the final assembly and painting. Though the first contract in 1975 included an option on the projected AV-16A the main provision was for six AV-8S, called Harrier Mk 55 in Britain and VA-1 Matador in Spain, plus two TAV-8S, Mk 58, VAE-1. In 1977 a repeat order was placed for five more AV-8S, and as Spain now had a more democratic form of government there was no problem and this deal was a straight buy from British Aerospace. The Matadors equip Essla (Escuadrilla) 008, whose home base is Rota but which has operated almost continuously from the old wooden deck of *Dédalo,* with conspicuous success.

Above left: Flapped STO by AV-8C during embarked trials aboard LHA-2 *Saipan* in October 1979./*MCAir*

Above: A fine picture of a Matador (Aircraft No 9) retracting gear after a rolling takeoff. Note radio altimeter aerials in ventral fin./*BAe*

Far left: Matador No 9 in the Dunsfold engine-running pen prior to delivery. Note the hold-down chains on each landing gear, and the extra broad VHF blade aerial (between the twin front pair behind the canopy and the tall tactical-VHF mast) added for communications compatibility with Armada helicopters./*BAe*

Below: USMC Harriers of VMA-542 from Cherry Point, NC seen aboard HMS *Hermes* during cross-deck operations./*MoD*

7 The Sea Harrier

Though mostly about a special version of the Harrier, this chapter also covers fixed-wing V/STOL at sea generally. But it cannot do so in depth; the subject is gigantic. Even the technology of flying a Harrier from a ship is one that already fills many large volumes.

Operation of rotating-wing V/STOLs from ships began in 1942 if not earlier, and in 1948 the US Navy studied prospects for fixed-wing V/STOL fighters that could operate from surface vessels. But the modern era of maritime V/STOL airpower really dawned on 9 February 1963, when Bill Bedford lifted off from Dunsfold in the first P.1127 and flew out to HMS *Ark Royal.* Since then Harriers have operated from more than 40 ships of nine navies, under almost every conceivable circumstance.

The early flying from *Ark,* which was at the invitation of a Royal Navy that had no idea it was soon to lose its conventional fixed-wing airpower, covered a great deal of new ground without the least difficulty, though Bedford had never flown aboard a ship previously. In 1966 ex-TES XV-6As briefly operated from USS *Independence* and *Raleigh,* while later that year a Kestrel aboard HMS *Bulwark* showed jet V/STOL and helicopter flying to be compatible on the same deck. The small deck of *Andrea Doria* was referred to in an earlier chapter. In 1969 a Harrier operated from USS *La Salle,* a command ship with a small aft platform, while another really set the world's navies talking by operating from the aft platform of HMS *Blake* while rolling $\pm 6°$ at sea with WOD (wind over the deck) gusting from 35 to 40 knots.

In 1970 Harriers flew Service Release trials from *Eagle,* clearing the way for RAF No 1 Sqn (landlubbers to a man) to go to sea in *Ark Royal.* Later in 1971 AV-8As completed BIS trials aboard an LPH *(Guadalcanal)* and LPD *(Coronado).* In 1972 a two-seater went aboard *Vikrant* of the Indian Navy and flew 22 sorties in two days in the tropical monsoon season. Later that year trials were flown from the wooden planks of *Dédalo,* as noted in the preceding chapter. In 1973 the French Navy invited a Harrier aboard the LPD *Jeanne d'Arc* and carrier *Foch.* The smallest jet-compatible decks so far are those of the Royal Fleet Auxiliaries *Olwen* and *Green Rover,* 55ft by 85ft. In the North Atlantic USMC squadron VMA-513 operated from USS *Guam* (then serving as the Interim Sea-Control Ship) in weather too severe for helicopter flying. Later, in 1974, this squadron again went aboard *Guam* for six months in the Mediterranean as part of the 6th Fleet's Amphibious Assault Force. In the course of this deployment the AV-8As also operated from carriers and from aft-platform LPDs.

In 1975 the Harrier GR.3 completed Release trials aboard *Ark,* with relevance to the uprated Pegasus and Sea Harrier. In September 1976 another Marine Corps squadron, VMA-231, embarked in the carrier *Franklin D. Roosevelt* for eight months with the 6th Fleet. In the course of this long deployment over 2,000 hours were flown in more than 2,000 missions, one-fifth at night, without a single accident or incident. The Navy crew of the carrier were impressed at the way the AV fitted into the ship's flying pattern, and the minimal demands the unique jets made on the carrier for launch or recovery. During this deployment the squadron flew across to *Guam* at short notice, steamed through the Suez Canal, flew in mass formation over Nairobi on Kenya's Independence Day and then rejoined *FDR* in the Med. This deployment was such splendid reading the report was suppressed by the US Navy Department.

This merely skates over the immense background of experience gained with the Harrier at sea. As early as 1972 Hawker Siddeley test pilots had defined the optimum techniques for different kinds of mission. The quickest reaction time is gained with VTO, less than 90 seconds from initiation of engine start to fully wing-borne being typical. VTO also removes the need for the ship to alter course or speed (except at very rare WOD speeds), burns least fuel (under 100lb to fully wing-borne flight), gives least sensitivity to deck motion and allows very rapid launch sequencing with each Harrier requiring a spot clearance radius of only 30 to 40 feet. STO, on the other hand, enables

Above right: In 1972 the civil G-VTOL flew 22 sorties in two days from INS *Vikrant* during the monsoon season./*Rolls-Royce*

Right: Ferranti's Blue Fox is one of the neatest radars around, working in I/J-band, monopulse, with flat aperture aerial. The whole set weighs less than 190lb./*Ferranti*

Resultant prototype tramlines
Harrier STO centre line (to avoid blast deflector ramp near bow)
Harrier wingtip safety line
Axial deck centre line of ship

Above: Two Hunter T.8Ms helped develop Blue Fox and are now serving as system trainers at RNAS Yeovilton. A third, and possibly a fourth, will be converted./*BAe*

Right: Three-view of the Sea Harrier FRS.1 with tanks and Sidewinders (nose fold shown in plan view)./*BAe*

Below right: The nav/attack system of the Sea Harrier is not only more comprehensive than that of land-based Harriers but also quite different. A fundamental advance is that it is digital./*BAe*

mission load to be increased, and John Farley and his colleagues worked out optimised ADD readings for ship STOs, making use of the fact that, unlike STO from land, the aircraft may safely sink after running off the end of the deck (when it is instantly out of ground effect). Deckrun and WOD can be traded, a typical case being a 500ft run and 30 knots WOD which gives just twice the payload limit for VTO. The deck runway width need be no more than 38.5 feet, the pilot steering along 'tram-lines' 7 feet apart. Landings are always vertical, so the normal operating mode is abbreviated as STOVL, short take-off and vertical landing.

Again, by 1972 various fundamental truths had been established for jet V/STOL from a ship at sea. No catapult, arrester wires or barrier are needed. The takeoff run is whatever the deck offers, and Harriers can line up nose-to-tail and make STO launches without problems due to the full-throttle aft-facing jets. Jet wash is no problem to men or equipment outside the runway safety line, though in VTO or VL aircraft should not overfly others. There is no problem with deck erosion or heating, and one could walk in bare feet over a steel deck immediately after a Harrier VTO or VL. Not least, in addition to opening up small and simple ships to high-performance airpower, jet V/STOL is demonstrably easier and safer than traditional fixed-wing carrier operations.

Having said all this, one marvels not that the Admiralty considered the Sea Harrier as far back as 1972 but that it took so long. Of course with Britain's closed style of government we cannot tell how far the decision to phase out conventional carriers and fixed-wing seagoing airpower reflected the future planning of the Admiralty, and Britain's withdrawal from global commitments, and how far it was imposed by an anti-defence Labour government against the Royal Navy's wishes. (In the same way, it is even now hard to discover how far the Sandys 'no more manned aircraft' was a nonsensical doctrine imposed on an unwilling RAF and how far it reflected the future planning of the RAF itself, as Sandys said it did.) When the P.1154RN was planned as the replacement for existing Fleet Air Arm fighter and attack aircraft it was intended it should be based aboard traditional carriers. Four were in commission – *Ark Royal, Eagle, Victorious* and *Hermes* – and a new ship, CVA-01, was about to be laid down. It seems to have been a major surprise to Their Lordships when the 1966 White Paper on Defence not only cancelled the new ship but announced the elimination of FAA fixed-wing airpower. Certainly the matelots did not take kindly to the idea, as witness the way the slogan FLY NAVY appeared across Britain.

The Royal Navy had had aeroplanes since 1911 and it is surely extraordinary that, when Hawker was allowed to see if a P.1127RAF was feasible, no murmur of interest emerged from the Admiralty. Like the RAF the naval aviators were steeped in big, traditional airpower, which had come to mean Mach 2. While the low-level attack mission might possibly be performed by a Harrier – though it was regarded at first as puny – the Navy had an important air-defence mission which called not only for interception radar but also for supersonic speed. This very unfortunately caused the full potential of the Harrier to be completely overlooked from 1965 until 1972, and even then it was another three years before any decision was taken. Bearing in mind the crippling erosion of capability due to inflation, this profligate

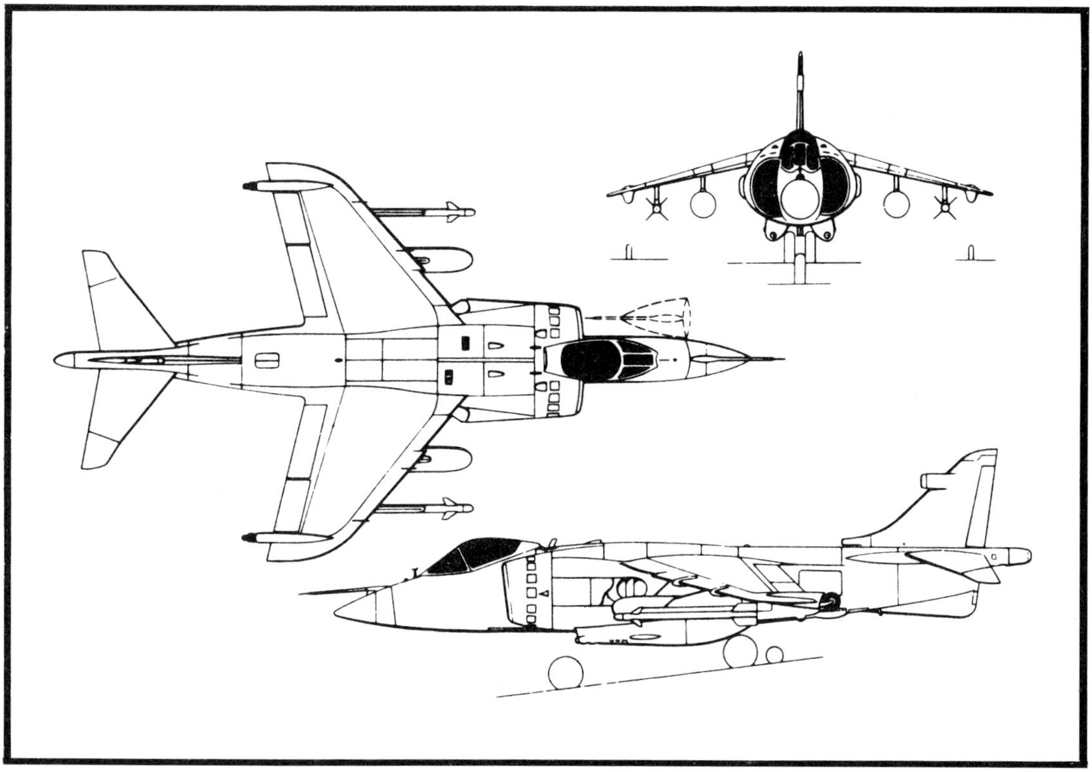

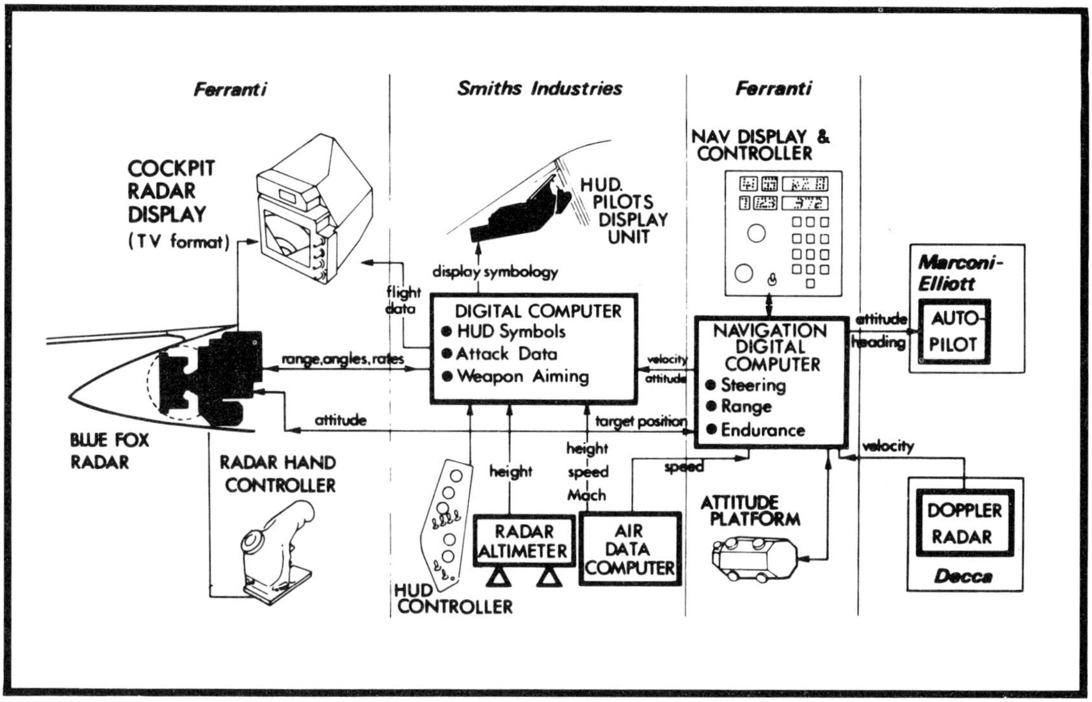

Ferranti
Smiths Industries
Ferranti
COCKPIT
RADAR
DISPLAY
(TV format)
HUD.
PILOTS
DISPLAY
UNIT
NAV DISPLAY &
CONTROLLER
display symbology
flight
data
DIGITAL COMPUTER
● HUD Symbols
● Attack Data
● Weapon Aiming
Marconi-
Elliott
NAVIGATION
DIGITAL
COMPUTER
● Steering
● Range
● Endurance
attitude
heading
AUTO-
PILOT
range,angles,rates
velocity
attitude
attitude
target position
BLUE FOX
RADAR
RADAR HAND
CONTROLLER
height
height
speed
Mach
speed
velocity
ATTITUDE
PLATFORM
RADAR
ALTIMETER
AIR
DATA
COMPUTER
DOPPLER
RADAR
Decca
HUD
CONTROLLER

Above: Sea Harriers first went to sea aboard HMS *Hermes* in 1979. Results were extremely good./*Rolls-Royce*

Below: HMS *Invincible* is now at sea with No 800 Sqn embarked. Here an aircraft of No 899 Sqn can just be seen against the funnel casing, while a plane-guard Sea King watches./*RNAS Culdrose*

Top right: While ship designers everywhere are drawing exciting jet V/STOL ships, with ski jumps at the bow or stern, a possibly more important idea is to prepare fast civilian container ships so that, in emergency, they could be Sea Harrier bases within a day or two. This is the BAe/Fairey Arapaho concept./*BAe*

Below right: Three-view of Sea Harrier FRS.1, without pylons./*BAe*

waste of time is to be regretted. For the record, the French planning was even worse: they rejected the Mach 1.6 Jaguar M and adopted the Super Etendard which is not only slower than a Harrier but also dependent upon traditional carriers and their deck machinery.

That a Maritime Harrier eventually came to pass is due both to the demonstrable impossibility of the small RAF Harrier force handling shipboard missions and to the farsighted vision of one or two naval officers. When the RN fixed-wing force was phased out, a widely-held supposition was that RAF Harriers would go to sea and take over the Fleet Air Arm's fixed-wing missions. So far as one can discover nothing was done to specify roles, missions or equipment for the RAF Harriers in such extra duties, but Hawker Siddeley did design two small modifications to clear Harriers for shipboard operation. One was to add tie-down shackles to the outrigger gears, and the other was to alter the wiring of the anti-skid brake system so that, when switched to off, the nosewheel steering is engaged, preventing the nosewheel from free castoring on a rolling deck. As previously noted, No 1 Sqn RAF was cleared for shipboard deployment in early 1971; but the impossibility of the three over-stretched Harrier squadrons also taking over the Fleet Air Arm's fixed-wing commitments, especially air defence of the Fleet at sea, seems eventually to have been understood.

General acceptance of a Royal Navy Harrier dates from early 1971. At first called the Maritime Support Harrier, it became known as the Maritime Harrier and finally was named Sea Harrier. At this time there were many attractive possibilities. Rolls-Royce, in possible partnership with Pratt & Whitney, proposed a refanned engine designated Pegasus 15, and in May 1972 a demonstrator Pegasus 15 ran at over 25,000 lb thrust at Bristol. Hawker Siddeley, in partnership with McDonnell Douglas, was engaged in studies for an advanced Harrier using this engine, and, as outlined in the next chapter, this became the AV-16A. There were several options for weapons and mission equipment, and a wide spectrum of available radars, most of them not British. Most of the possibilities were thrashed out at meetings in 1971-2, but the dominant feature of these all-British talks was that there was no money. The RAF and RN had overspent, neither was eager to cut existing programmes to sponsor a Maritime Harrier, and government funding was not offered. A further complication was that there were many possible sizes and configurations for the associated ship.

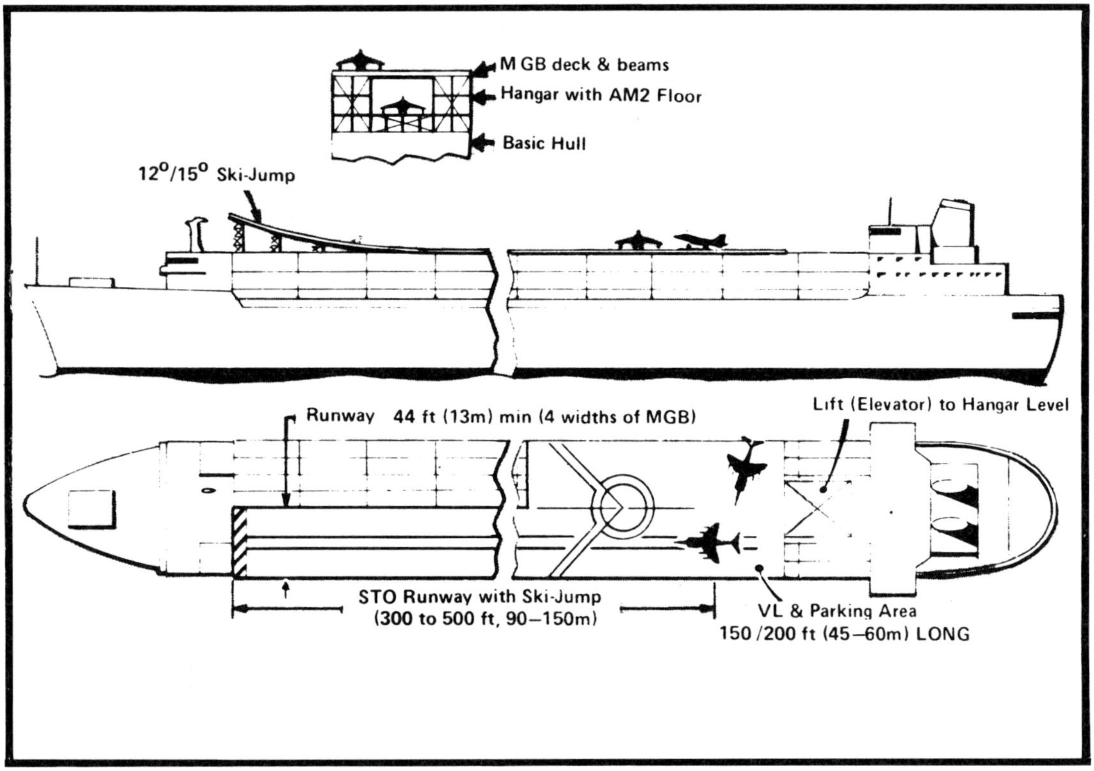
M GB deck & beams
Hangar with AM2 Floor
Basic Hull
12°/15° Ski-Jump
Runway 44 ft (13m) min (4 widths of MGB)
Lift (Elevator) to Hangar Level
STO Runway with Ski-Jump
(300 to 500 ft, 90–150m)
VL & Parking Area
150 /200 ft (45–60m) LONG

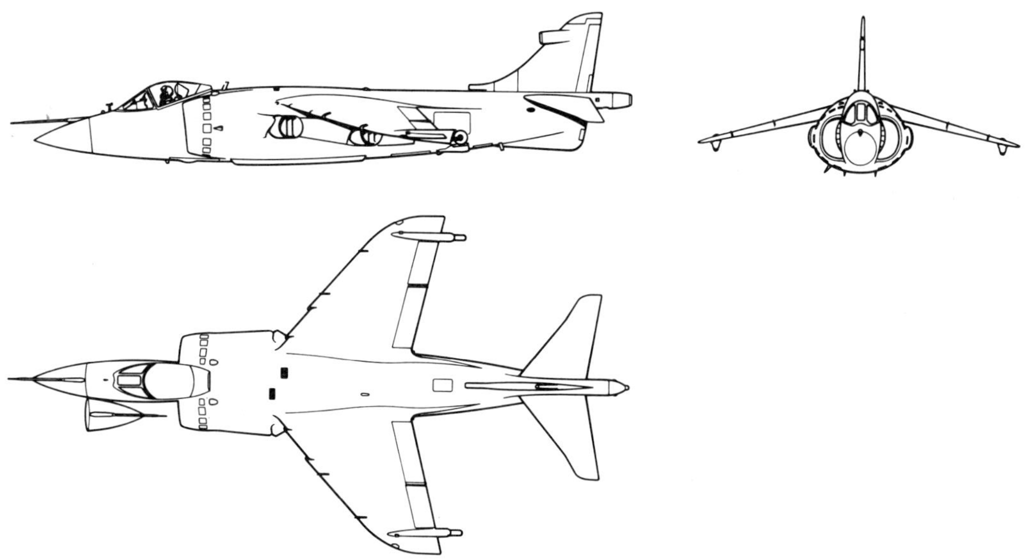

As at that time the notion of fixed-wing carriers in Britain was still taboo the ship was given the odd title of through-deck cruiser (TDC). As early as 1969 the RN Ship Department at Bath had begun detailed studies for a new class of so-called cruiser of about 20,000 tons, basically similar to the USS *Iwo Jima* with an island bridge structure and through (ie unbroken from stern to stem) deck. It was said they would have three main capabilities: deployment of ASW (anti-submarine warfare) helicopters, command/control of naval and maritime-air forces, and 'a contribution to area air defence'. It was the last bit that was unexplained, and two years later, when Vickers at Barrow were well into ship design under contract, it was still 'unknown' whether the Harrier or any V/STOL would be suitable for shipboard use. Why this was not known was never explained, but a clue may be afforded by the 1970 *Brassey's Annual* which said, of the Harrier, 'The present model has too short an endurance to enable it to fulfil the functions of a shipborne aircraft'.

This belief was mistaken, as the fuel capacity of today's Sea Harrier is the same as it was in 1970, but there were clearly powerful unexplained factors working against the acceptance of a Maritime Harrier. One of the main reasons for slow progress was undoubtedly a major inter-Service battle between the high-level planning staffs in MoD(RN) and MoD (Air). Certainly the Royal Air Force saw the re-emergence of a fixed-wing Fleet Air Arm as a threat to its share of the rapidly diminishing Defence Vote. Very properly it questioned the strategic requirement for the 'See Through Carrier' in a streamlined Royal Navy whose role was supposedly confined to NATO. In particular it was highly sceptical – and in this it was joined by not a few Naval officers – of the survivability of any largish slow surface ship in the age of the high-speed nuclear-propelled attack submarine and the sophisticated homing missile.

The RAF was particularly sceptical about the Navy's claim that it needed the new ships and the Sea Harriers to provide for 'air defence of the Fleet'. 'What Fleet?', some light-blue cynics not unreasonably asked; but, that apart, the RAF scepticism was well-placed. How much air defence was likely to be provided by a clutch of three or four subsonic Sea Harriers against a threat that would almost certainly include missile-armed supersonic Backfire bombers? Moreover, what little 'air defence' was provided would be 'point-defence' of the Harriers' own base and its immediate vicinity – a very wasteful use of expensive air power, and virtually impossible to integrate into a more sophisticated area system. Even more worrying to the RAF planners of the day was the thought that gullible politicians, believing that the Navy could defend itself from air attack in UK offshore waters, might cut the RAF's role in NATO Area 12, and with it the requirement to develop an air-defence variant of the MRCA – later known as Tornado. Possibly the diehards still insisted the crew had to include an observer (navigator). Suffice to say that in August 1972 a Naval Staff Target was finally issued which not only represented the rebirth of the fixed-wing Fleet Air Arm but also was actually written around the existing Harrier airframe. The budget situation was such that it was a take-it-or-leave-it chance of buying a V/STOL changed as little as possible from that already in production. The contract for completion of the TDC design was placed in the same year, and in April 1973 Vickers received the contract for construction of the first ship, later named *Invincible* (incidentally, never before the name of a carrier). The TDC apellation gradually faded into disuse, being replaced by Command Class cruiser, AS (anti-submarine cruiser) or CAH (Carrier, Assault Helicopter).

In November 1972 Hawker received a contract for the Sea Harrier design study and development cost plan. As the original staff target had, for cost reasons, been based on what could be achieved with no major change to the Harrier other than its equipment, the work could have been speedy. Sadly the halting progress grew, if anything, worse as the months ticked by. A trickle of funding just held the Kingston team together until in December 1973 the company at last heard the long awaited go-ahead was to be announced the following week. Instead the Commons was engrossed with the Fuel Crisis, soaring inflation and the Three-Day Week, leading in 1974 to a new Labour administration whose main interest with Defence was to see what could be cancelled. The only progress in 1973 was an award to Rolls-Royce to develop the Pegasus 104 and one to Ferranti for Blue Fox. The Pegasus 104 is a Mk 103 with some material changes (for example, the fan casing is aluminium instead of magnesium/zirconium), sacrificial corrosion protection and an increased-capacity gearbox. Blue Fox is perhaps the most important single new item in the Sea Harrier and it is one of the best radars in any small maritime aircraft. Derived from the same maker's Seaspray, used in naval Lynx helicopters, it is likewise a frequency-agile monopulse set with electronic scanning and good versatility for use in hostile ECM/ECCM environments in both the air/air and air/surface modes. Inflation wrecked the hope that radar information could be presented on the HUD, so the display is a head-down daylight-viewing box with TV raster presentation.

In 1974 the near-zero progress seemed to slow further, and by spring 1975 many people in industry

Top: Any pilot of a Harrier or AV-8A will appreciate the markedly different 'office' of the Sea Harrier; a portion has been blanked off for reasons of security. CCS=communications control system./*BAe*

Above: This inboard profile of the FRS.1 shows the radar, some of the items added under the cockpit and the two rear-fuselage bays occupied by electronics and air-conditioning. The pilot can see rearwards above the inlet on each side in the Sea Harrier./*BAe*

Right: First flight of a Sea Harrier, by the third aircraft still in its primer paint in August 1978./*BAe*

Top left: AV-8A Harriers of VMA-513, the first USMC squadron to form on the type, securely tied down to the deck of USS *Guam* during Interim Sea Control Ship tests in January 1972./*US Navy*

Top right: Sea Harrier FRS.1 of No 801 Naval Air Sqn (NAS) at RNAS Yeovilton in February 1981./*Denis Calvert*

Above: The first front line squadron to form on the Sea Harrier was No 800 NAS, one of whose aircraft is seen here with the 'H' fin code denoting its assignment to HMS *Hermes*./*Denis Calvert*

Left: Sea Harriers of the Fleet Air Arm's trials squadron, No 700A, aboard HMS *Hermes* in November 1979./*Danny du Fell*

had given up hope. Then on 15 May 1975 Defence Minister Roy Mason suddenly announced that the RN was to acquire 24 Sea Harriers, to operate from three of the through-deck ships. The news came over the BBC and John Fozard, then chief designer (Harrier), and chief test pilot John Farley were told by Dunsfold tower as they were on short finals in the company Dove!

Probably no aircraft in history has had so long and needlessly delayed a gestation. Even then Hawker did not get an Instruction to Proceed until well into June, but by that time all the basic design was understood and detail work had started. Almost all the effort was devoted to creating a new front end; hardly anything else was altered. Whereas in 1963 the RN view was that the P.1154 was a non-starter because it was a single-seater, by the mid-70s the validity of a single-seat aircraft was unquestioned. But the man in the seat had a lot to do, and to ease his work-load and accommodate a considerably augmented nav/attack installation with more comprehensive cockpit displays the decision was taken as far back as 1972 to redesign the forward fuselage with the seat and canopy raised by about 11 inches. As a bonus this gives much better all-round view, and also allows the pilot to check the outrigger gears which in the Harrier are masked by inlets.

It was agreed that there would be no Sea Harrier prototype, all 24 aircraft being built in production tooling. The first three, XZ438-440, were to be instrumented for manufacturer's flight test and development, and first flight was set for July 1977. Meanwhile, much work had already been done on the new systems, notably the radar. Ferranti's Electronic Systems Department not only had the Seaspray as a starting point but also the experience of intercept and attack radars for the Lightning, Buccaneer and TSR.2 (and would have supplied radars for both versions of P.1154). The requirement was for air intercept and air/surface-vessel search and strike. This called for four airborne operating modes: search, with a Sector (B-type) scan or PPI with multi-bar or single scan; attack, with lead-pursuit or chase in the air-combat mission and weapon-aiming via the HUD in surface attack; boresight, for ranging on targets of opportunity; and xpdr (transponder) for the identification of friendly radar returns. Blue Fox operates in I-band (previously called X-band) and like all modern sets is made up of line-replaceable modules with built-in test and MTBF (mean time between failures) planned in 1972 for 100 hours, predicted in 1978 at 120 and actually coming out nearer 300. The trim 186lb package was first flown on 9 January 1978 in a Hunter T.8M, one of two two-seat Hunters rebuilt by Hawker Siddeley at Brough with the complete Sea Harrier nav/attack system. Initially used for systems development, one at Dunsfold and the other at Bedford with the Royal Signals and Radar Research Establishment, they are now serving as system trainers with the RN. In addition, in 1974 Hawker flew a P.1127RAF, XV277, with a metal mock-up radar nose, but this could not be representative of the final shape which goes with the raised cockpit. Another change in the definitive form is relocation of the long pitot boom above the nose somewhat resembling the arrangement on the Harrier GR.3 with laser nose.

Raising the cockpit provided 11 inches extra depth under the floor, more space on the side consoles and greater depth behind the front panel, all of which has been used to the full. In addition the seat is the faster-acting Mk 10A, taking only 1.5 sec from initiation to full parachute deployment. Another important change is that, as well as giving 360° view horizontally, the canopy is bulged to give a rather better view downwards. As noted in the last chapter, this cockpit and canopy may be used on any future RAF Harriers.

An accompanying block diagram shows the totally different and more comprehensive avionics. Inevitably the switch has been made to all-digital processing in place of analog, and there are separate computers for navigation, attack and weapon-aiming (via the HUD) and air-data. The HUD itself has greater versatility, especially for the air/air role, and the lens and reflector plate are larger than in previous Harriers. Symbology and graphic inputs are supplied by a 20,000-word computer. An 8,000-word computer ties together the navigation system which, to avoid alignment problems at sea, is no longer pure-inertial. It comprises a master attitude reference related to that of Tornado but with lower-cost (not INS-quality) gyros, with output monitored by Decca Type 72 doppler. This gives accuracy as good as that of a Harrier for about the same system cost but with greater flexibility and without the need for pure-inertial techniques. (At the same time the author has no doubt of the viability of these techniques at sea, which were abundantly explored aboard *Eagle* in 1970 and *Guam* in 1972 and today can be tied to other navaids such as Omega.)

The rest of the Sea Harrier is almost unchanged, and the landing gears in particular needed no beefing-up though a small change was to add lashing lugs. To match the increased side area of the nose the fin was enlarged by building in the RWR as an extra section 5 inches deep. The tailplane nose-up travel is extended 2° and the roll-control RCVs at the wingtips are enlarged to give even more powerful control in possible turbulence in ship wakes. The wheel brakes have an emergency system for use in confined spaces, the engine water-injection can operate for longer periods (for example, during a protracted approach in a heavy sea) and not only is magnesium avoided in the airframe but special marine paint coatings are used. To reduce pilot workload, especially with radar in use, the flight controls are not only autostabilised but a simple autopilot function is added, giving heading, height and turn hold. Electrics and hydraulics are both considerably revised, and the lox (liquid oxygen) system is by a different supplier (British Oxygen) and of a different type. The engine drives more powerful alternators, mainly because of the radar, and the nozzles are stressed for viffing. The main leg incorporates a holdback anchor; originally it was intended to engage with a hydraulically snubbed arrester in the deck, the pilot severing the tie after confirming correct engine thrust and the deck party retrieving the tie-rod for re-use. The ventral fin contains a radar altimeter.

While the Sea Harriers were taking shape, a completely new idea made ship (or any other) vectored-thrust V/STOL even more attractive. It was so blindingly obvious that it took a genius to think of it; Lt-Cdr Doug Taylor, RN, has so many novel ideas that a few are bound to come off. He proposed that V/STOL ships should have what soon became known as a 'ski jump', an upward curvature at the end of the STO run to impart a positive vertical velocity to the aircraft. The basic advantage is that much heavier fuel or weapon loads can be lifted from a given deck run; or the same mission can be flown from an even smaller and cheaper ship. An important secondary advantage is enhanced safety.

In the normal STO the aircraft accelerates at full power with nozzles aft and at the takeoff point (in a ship, the end of the deck) the nozzles are rotated to the 50° stop. This gives enough lift, together with that already generated by the wing, to support the weight; the residual forward thrust component gives increasing airspeed. With a ski jump the curving upward semi-ballistic trajectory means that the aircraft can leave the end of wheel support, at the end of the curved ramp, at a much lower speed, say 60 kt instead of 90 kt. With nozzles at 50° there is still not enough lift to support the aircraft, but as it arches upward it flies ever-faster and after 10 seconds levels out at the required airspeed. Moreover, by this time it is not at deck height but at about 200 feet. This means that, should there be total engine failure in the first few seconds of flight, the pilot has much longer in which to recognise the situation and eject than the 2 seconds in a flat launch at deck height. While a cat launch of a CTOL aircraft can be fired while the ship is in the bows-up part of her pitch cycle, a V/STOL takeoff takes longer and could conceivably be timed so that the aircraft left the front end of the deck at the worst point in the pitch cycle, literally pointing down at the sea. With a ski jump there is always a positive vertical velocity even in this unlikely eventuality. Ski jumps make great sense in land operations, but have not yet been made easily portable.

The first ski ramp was a big adjustable installation built by British Steel (Redpath Dorman Long) at RAE Bedford, the first Harrier ski takeoff being on 5 August 1977 at a 6° exit angle. By December 1977 a 12° angle was being tested, with endspeeds at maximum weight as low as 75 knots – an amazing 65 knots less than for a runway STO takeoff. By this time every pilot who could find an excuse had flown a ski-jump takeoff – the total soon exceeded 100, by day and night, in over 1,000 launches – and trials included 15° and 17½° at speeds down to 42 knots before finishing at 20° at which the Harrier oleos were just bottoming because of the 4 g normal acceleration. Most unfortunately, though nobody could claim the ski-jump trials were protracted, the first two Command cruisers *Invincible* and *Illustrious* were designed with a Sea Dart SAM on the centreline at the bow, virtually their only armament, and this has restricted the ramp to a mere 7°. The third ship, *Ark Royal,* will have a 12° ramp right at the bows. Another ski-equipped ship is *Hermes,* a CAH, also with a 12° installation. Not yet reflected in published ship designs is the smaller size of vessel that can operate Sea Harriers using this immensely rewarding technique. Bearing in mind that endspeed is squared to give the deck run, it can be seen that, at a guess, a 5,000-ton ship could embark Sea Harriers, if designed from the start for such a role.

Construction of the first Sea Harriers was delayed by industrial unrest and other problems unconnected with the aircraft. Eventually the third machine, XZ450, overtook the others and made the first flight, unpainted, on 20 August 1978. Painted, it did 15° ski launches at the Farnborough show two weeks later, on a sagging catenary by Fairey Engineering based on the Medium Girder Bridge. XZ451 was handed over to the RN on 18 June 1979, and the Intensive Flying Trials Unit, 700A Sqn, commissioned at Yeovilton on 19 September 1979. A month later this unit joined *Hermes* with two aircraft, plus two more from Boscombe Down and a fifth from Dunsfold, for an outstandingly successful sea trial (G-VTOL also participated). The programme included day and night flying with all weapon options and in strong crosswinds or deliberate mistrim of the aircraft. All the 126 landings were vertical, one of them with 1,000lb bombs on the outer pylons.

Today 700A has become 899 Harrier HQ Sqn, training pilots and co-ordinating the standards and doctrines for the three seagoing front-line units, Nos 800-802 Sqns. No 800 Sqn, traditionally the RN's crack aviation unit, commissioned in April 1980 and embarked aboard *Invincible* in January 1981. In the same month No 801 was commissioned, and before this book appears will have relieved 800 aboard *Invincible;* 800 will have joined *Hermes* after her refit and addition of a ski jump. Earlier, in 1980, *Hermes* had been the first of the four V/STOL ships fitted with HAPI (Harrier approach path indicator), devised by Dr Reg Dawson at the Admiralty Surface Weapons Establishment and Tony Smith at RAE Bedford. A red/white optical system, it comprises two units on the left side of the deck and a CAI (close approach indicator) 28 feet above the deck on the left side of the superstructure.

In May 1978 a further ten aircraft were ordered, bringing the RN total to 34, of which 14 had flown by April 1980 and 26 a year later. Because this aircraft gives real capability from small, simple ships it has generated global interest – startlingly more than the Harrier itself – and the first of many anticipated orders was placed by the Indian Navy in December 1979 (it was not announced until June 1980, and the recipient was not identified). Six Sea Harrier FRS.51s were ordered, to a standard almost identical to the FRS.1, together with two navalized Harrier T.60 trainers. In 1984 came the expected repeat order of ten FRS.51 and two more T.60 aircraft. They operate with INS.300 'Leopard' squadron from shore bases and from INS *Vikrant.*

Three views of No 801 NAS aboard HMS *Invincible* in June 1981. /*Denis Calvert*

8
The AV-8B

Ten years ago seems like a prehistoric era in which inflation was a relatively minor problem, so that it was logical to develop aircraft in the traditional way. By 1970, therefore, Hawker's project team had already carried out studies into advanced developments of the Harrier. In 1971 it was joined by McDonnell Aircraft (MCAir), while the Rolls-Royce Bristol team linked up with Pratt & Whitney on advanced Pegasi (if that plural is not pedantic). Sadly, it was all to come unstuck. The one good thing to come out of it was an American aircraft which is the subject of this chapter.

Most of the Kingston studies were done under the project number of P.1184 and 1185, popularly called Super Harrier. Extra thrust seemed essential. Kingston did not have to make much hardware, though by 1972 models were being tested in tunnels; but Bristol did decide to build a demonstrator engine to show the performance possible with the Pegasus 15. This was planned as a low-cost, low-risk engine using as many existing parts as possible but with a fan increased in diameter by 2¼ inches, representing the limiting size that could be accommodated in the Harrier fuselage. This greatly increased mass flow, which is roughly proportional to the square of inlet diameter, and so called for enlarged inlets and ducts, in turn requiring modified Harrier fuselage frames. Apart from this the engine was little different and, at company expense, a representative Pegasus 15 fan was built on to an existing core. The design thrust of the definitive engine was 24,500lb, so the engine designers were pleased to record 24,900lb with this crude lash-up in May 1972. This augured extremely well for the next V/STOL generation, and in fact, 25,000lb thrust was assumed by both Hawker and MCAir in their studies.

Predictably the RAF showed little interest, because of lack of money; all it had in mind was a long-term plan for a Harrier replacement. But the Marine Corps was interested in an advanced Harrier as a replacement for the A-4, while the US Navy had a range of possible requirements, notably the Hipaas (high-performance attack aircraft system) and a multi-role V/STOL fighter for use aboard the Sea Control Ships, a new class of extremely advanced versatile ships of 11,000 to 16,000 tons able to operate jet V/STOLs and helicopters as well as deploy other systems. As noted in the preceding chapter the Royal Navy was also coming round to appreciate the possible value of a Maritime Harrier, so the prospects were good for a really big next-generation programme.

At government level a Joint Management Committee was set up with co-chairmen (Rear-Admiral D. K. Weitzenfeld USN and D. J. Harper of Mintech), project managers (Col R. C. Marsh USMC and Air Cdre E. Burchmore), financial specialists (C. L. Davis and A. Chinneck) and engine specialists (A. S. Atkinson and J. Forshaw). This board was the interface between the four customers (USN, USMC, RAF and RN) and the four industrial companies (HSA, MCAir, R-R and PWA). With the concurrence of Naval Air Systems Command, MCAir raised two new designations to follow the AV-8A: AV-8B for the existing two-seater, and AV-8C (later AV-16A) for the proposed Advanced Harrier with the Pegasus 15. The basic assumption agreed by all parties was that the new aircraft would have a redesigned wing, and be able to carry mission avionics and weapons specified by the four customers, but would otherwise be a minimum-cost, minimum-change derivative of the Harrier/AV-8A.

This was a crucially important point in the entire story, not only of the Harrier but of the effective military strength of the West. The possibility of perhaps 2,000-plus related Advanced Harrier type aircraft configured for four launch customers and many foreign buyers was obvious. But there were small seeds that were to grow and destroy the whole programme. By far the largest was the self-centred outlook of the US political machine, which traditionally and instinctively resisted anything tainted with the label 'foreign'. Second, the general view in the Defense Department was that the Hawker V/STOL idea was simple, crude and old-fashioned; instead of recognising that the simplicity was its

Right: One of the might-have-beens was the HSA/MCAir AV-16A, seen here configured for the USMC, RAF, RN and USN. It would have had a long-span supercritical wing and Pegasus 15 engine of 25,000lb thrust. Moral: if you delay decisions long enough, inflation makes them impossible anyway./*Rolls-Royce*

NAVY
ROYAL NAVY

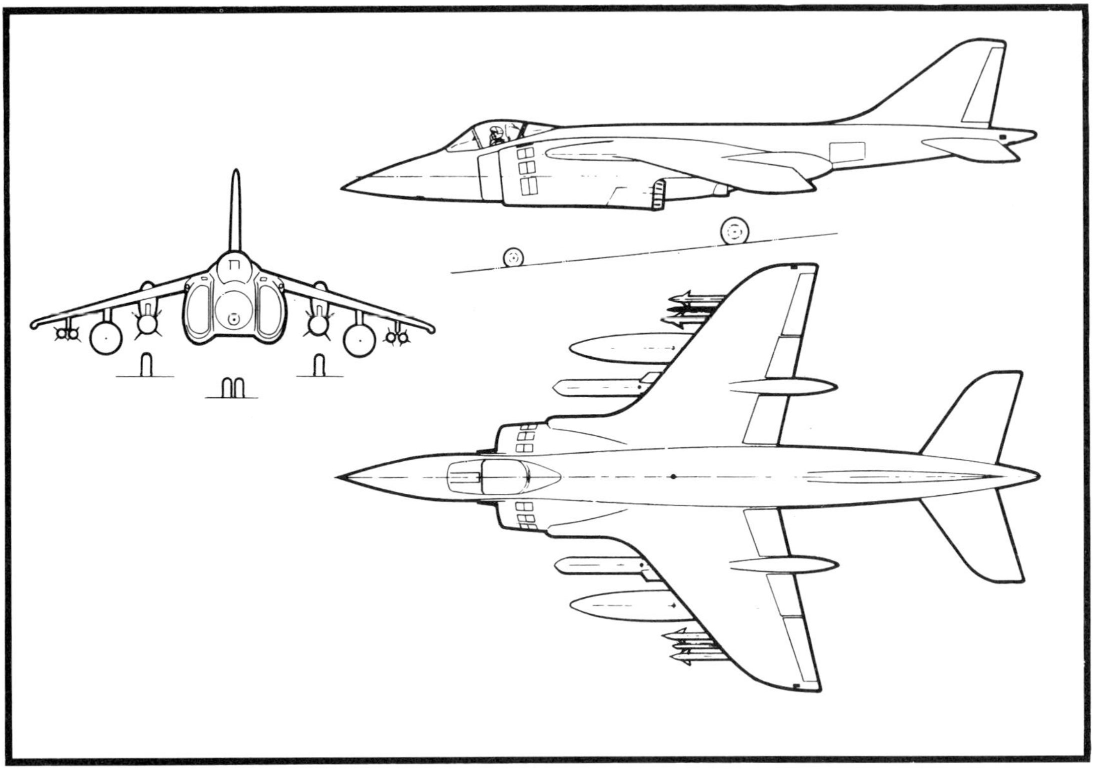

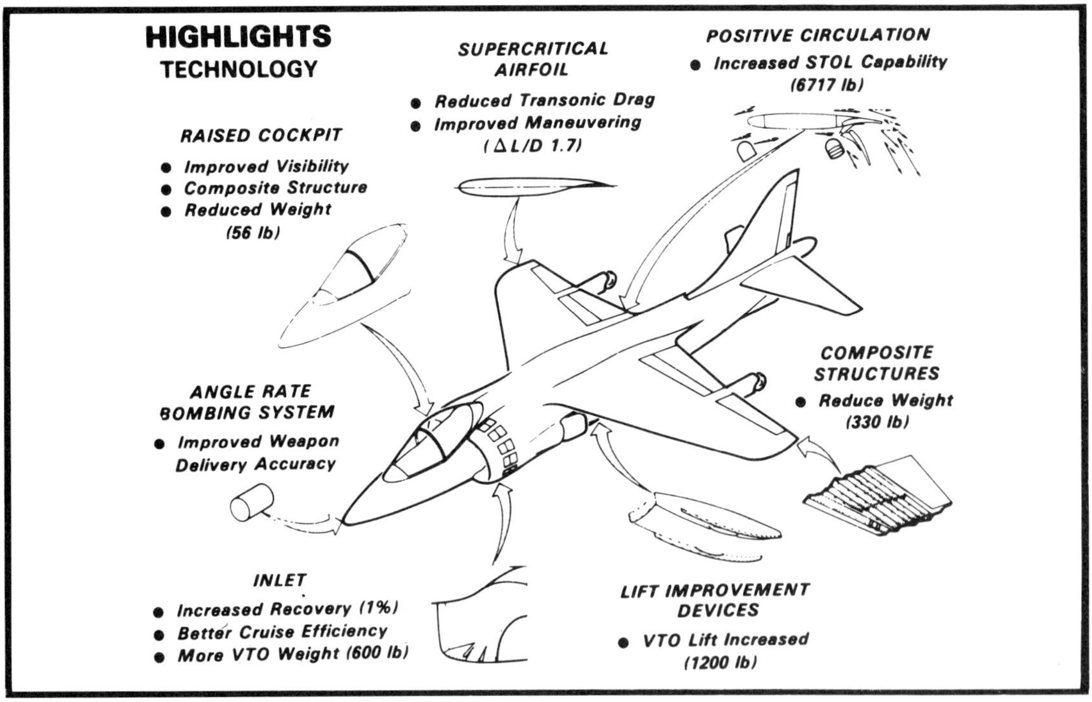
HIGHLIGHTS
TECHNOLOGY
SUPERCRITICAL AIRFOIL
● Reduced Transonic Drag
● Improved Maneuvering (ΔL/D 1.7)
POSITIVE CIRCULATION
● Increased STOL Capability (6717 lb)
RAISED COCKPIT
● Improved Visibility
● Composite Structure
● Reduced Weight (56 lb)
ANGLE RATE BOMBING SYSTEM
● Improved Weapon Delivery Accuracy
COMPOSITE STRUCTURES
● Reduce Weight (330 lb)
INLET
● Increased Recovery (1%)
● Better Cruise Efficiency
● More VTO Weight (600 lb)
LIFT IMPROVEMENT DEVICES
● VTO Lift Increased (1200 lb)

strength, so that it alone would succeed, it regarded anything of this ilk as small and interim. The main effort by Navair was to fund later V/STOL ideas by US industry, and in particular ideas which it considered better suited to supersonic flight than a turbofan of large frontal area with a 'four-poster' nozzle system.

A secondary problem was the wealth of possibilities. The preferred minimum-change aircraft was a Harrier or AV-16A with a Pegasus 15 and a wing of longer span and more area, housing more fuel. There were also many small things that could be done to augment lift, or reduce losses, and thus carry heavier loads of weapons or fuel even on the existing engine. The basic wing had a deep supercritical section and long span tailored to existing missions and offering much higher performance except in speed, which might even be slightly reduced. In the longer term Navair wanted a supersonic aircraft for the Sea Control Ship, and asked Kingston how such a machine should be designed. The Rolls project engineers began producing brochures on a Pegasus 15 with PCB to be rated at 34,500lb – more even than the BS.100/9.

Above left: The ultimate form of AV-16 was the all-British S-6, one of a series of supersonic proposals which departed ever further from the existing Harrier but capitalised on the P.1154./*BAe*

Below left: Dating from 1977 this diagram outlines some of the major ways in which McDonnell Aircraft turned the AV-8A into the AV-8B./*MCAir*

Below: This diagram showing a Harrier hovering near the ground helps explain how the central fountain can suck down, be reingested and – with proper airframe changes – greatly increase lift./*BAe*

Doubtless the Navair assessors did their best to make the correct choice for the SCS V/STOL but, as one reads the reports, it becomes obvious that the AV-8C was not really considered. It was thought to be a brute-force approach which also relied heavily upon pilot skill; what Navair wanted was something with clever augmentation of the lift jets, combined with black-box automatic control and packaged in an airframe which, when the propulsion system was switched to the forward-flight mode, was suitable for Mach 2. On 13 October 1972 Navair awarded the contract to North American Rockwell for the XFV-12A, a concept that fitted the Navy's thinking exactly. (Anything more remote from what the Marines wanted would be hard to find.) It was expected that the first XFV-12A would demonstrate vertical lift in August 1974 and fly in the CTOL mode the following month. As I write, in 1981, we are still waiting for either event; the whole thing has become an embarrassment. Congress has so far not been roused in the way it would have been had a 'foreign airplane' been chosen in 1972, despite the fact that many times the planned sum has been spent and the US Navy has little to show beyond a lot of V/STOL know-how that mostly could have been obtained from Kingston.

Undaunted, MCAir and Hawker continued their studies, and predictably kept finding ways to make the Advanced Harrier better. By 1973 called AV-8+ or AV-8-Plus, it grew a wider fuselage because the engine had grown not by 2¼ inches but by 2¾, partly to enable 25,000lb to be achieved at reduced gas temperatures for longer life. Royal Navy Maritime Harrier studies fed in the raised cockpit, for all-round view and to allow an avionics-packed nose. The enlarged inlets were reprofiled, and fitted with a double row of suck-in auxiliary doors around each duct instead of a single row. Both airframe companies

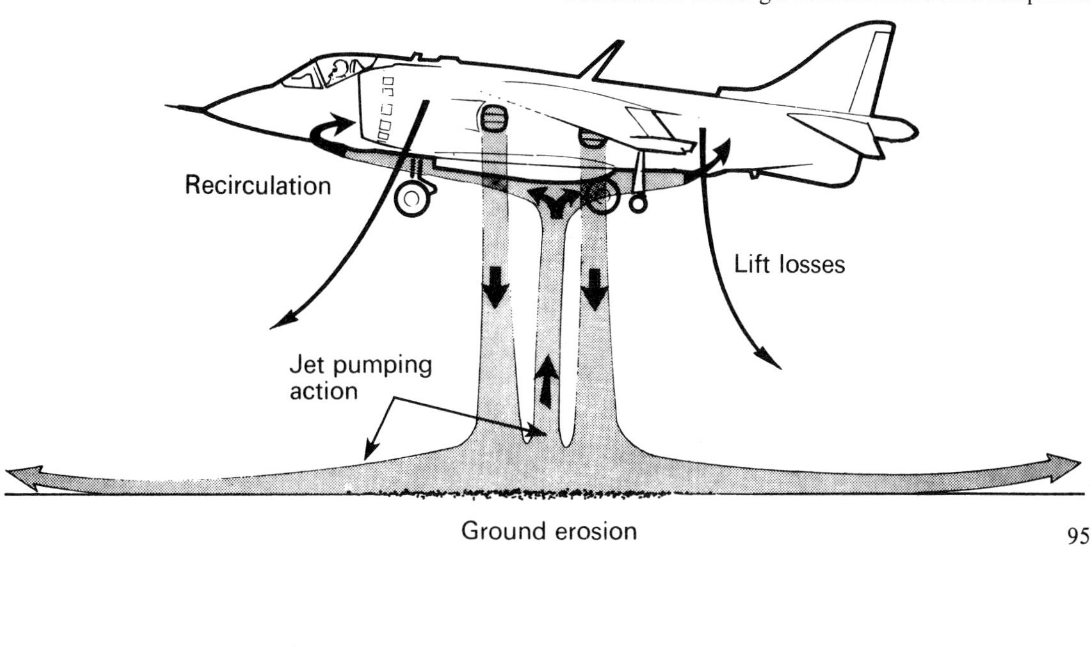

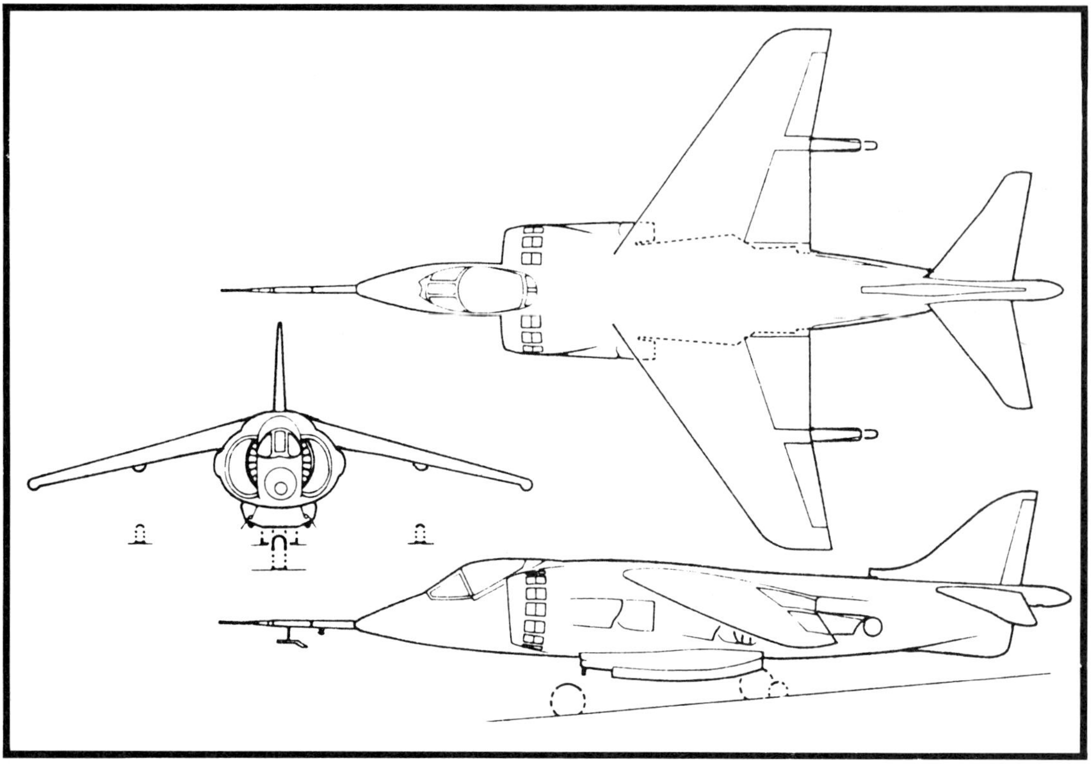

designed advanced supercritical wings, models of which were tested in the 11-foot tunnel at NASA Ames. A one-fifth-scale front fuselage and inlets was tested in the hovering mode in the PTF (Propulsion Test Facility) at Naval Air Station Trenton, NJ. It boiled up to a climax on 13 December 1973 when the Project Definition for what had been rechristened the AV-16A was submitted to the two governments.

While this proposal was evaluated, the British partner companies continued in 1974 with the AV-16 S series, S standing for supersonic. The S-1 had PCB for V/STOL, the S-2 a new wing, and by the S-6 there was not much Harrier left but the maker's name. The thin wing had short span, compared with the supercritical AV-16A. The body was slimmer and longer. The tail was completely new. The engine was a 15PCB with further changes, including a new nozzle geometry as described in the final chapter. For this reason the main gears went back to the P.1154RN solution in being mounted on the wings, folding into downstream fairings. Speed at altitude was Mach 1.95; but the customers stayed away. The US Navy had picked Rockwell, the Marines wanted the simple subsonic machine, the RAF was uncertain, and the RN thought itself daring even in considering the basic Maritime Harrier. By 1975 the work was in a low key. The partners were in disarray, and Britain's Labour government capitalised on the fact.

The 1975 Defence White Paper, presented on 19 March by Roy Mason, was mainly a string of cuts. Almost unnoticed by the media was the statement that 'there is not enough common ground on the Advanced Harrier for us to join in the programme with the US'. As always in Britain's secret environment we shall not be told for a long time how far this was the view of those who wanted to have an Advanced Harrier and how far it was just an excuse by politicians looking for easy cuts. What perhaps was beyond Mr Mason's range of vision was that this was to lose many years in a field in which time is not on the side of the West, and particularly not on the side of Britain, and that in the long term it could even yet bring about the collapse of the one field of British military aircraft design in which the nation still holds a lead.

The announcement dismayed the world's No 1 jet V/STOL team. Though morale was boosted by the go-ahead on the Sea Harrier two months later, that merely broadened the base of the programme. Nothing was said about further progress of the basic concept to meet the growing needs of what should before long encompass almost all the world's air

Left: Three-view of the two YAV-8B aircraft./*MCAir*

Above: The first 'AV-8B' to be rolled out was this mock-up, based on a crashed AV-8A, photographed at St Louis on 7 August 1975. /*MCAir*

Right: One of the more unusual tests on new aircraft types is to see how the airframe behaves when struck by simulated lightning. This AV-8B model was taking pulses of up to 200,000 amperes in 1980. /*MCAir*

Below: Next came this outdoor test, followed by testing in the 40 by 80 foot tunnel at NASA Ames Research Center. The front nozzles have yet to change./*MCAir*

Below right: The completely new wing of the AV-8B is still the largest carbon-fibre primary structure flying, weighing 1,374lb with its movable surfaces. The first YAV-8B is seen here in March 1978. /*MCAir*

Right: From the side the AV-8B does not look very different from other Harriers. This is the No 1 YAV-8B./*MCAir*

Centre left: 9 November 1978, and the first YAV-8B is seen hovering at St Louis International Airport in the hands of company pilot C. A. Plummer./*MCAir*

Centre right: Differences are more marked when the span of the wing can be seen; here No 1 YAV makes a neat vertical recovery during its first shipboard trials aboard LHA-2 *Saipan* in October 1979./*MCAir*

Bottom right: An April 1979 photograph at the US Naval Air Test Center, Patuxent River, showing both YAV-8Bs as well as two As, a TAV and a Learjet./*MCAir*

forces (when they wake up) later in this century. What happened in Britain is the subject of the next chapter. Tragically, from 19 March 1975 what happened in Britain has been only distantly related to what has happened in the USA. As far as hardware is concerned the United States has virtually taken over the programme, while the original team has done its best to salvage what it can.

Though not entirely surprised, the Americans were also disheartened by Mr Mason's decision. Working together the two nations could accomplish things not even the United States could afford alone, and in particular the unique experience of Patchway on the engine and Kingston on the airframe removed the element of risk that would be bound to attend unilateral American efforts. But Americans seldom let grass grow under their feet, and even before Mr Mason's announcement discussions had been held to sort out the possibilities following a British withdrawal. Pratt & Whitney did not wish unilaterally to take on major development of the Pegasus, and what killed the AV-16A was the costing to US qualification of the Pegasus 15 at $600 million, or $200,000 per extra pound of thrust! Subsequent US work was predicated on whatever engine Rolls-Royce could offer. In effect it boiled down to using the existing engine, though, as noted later, small improvements are available and there is a possibility of an engine with fractionally higher performance. But from early in the P.1127 story the nozzles were regarded as airframe, and even in these seemingly simple parts MCAir was able to effect a major improvement.

Before anything could be planned MCAir had to know the requirement and possible numbers for customers, and in the Fiscal Year 1975, which ended on 30 June 1975, the US Navy gave its agreement in principle to a programme for a proposed new AV-8B version (the original two-seater becoming the TAV-8A) numbering 342 aircraft, all for the Marine Corps, but with the verbally expressed possibility of a follow-on batch of roughly the same size for the Navy itself. The AV-8B was to be the best aircraft possible using the existing Pegasus 11, incorporating any of the advances studied in the AV-16A project. MCAir had a licence to develop the Harrier as well as build it, and was not even obliged to continue to work with Kingston. But it was sensible to continue collaboration, and the UK team, called British Aerospace from 1977, remained responsible for approximately one-third of the airframe (the portion behind the engine) and is a candidate to bid for production. But MCAir took over basic responsibility for the new AV-8B as prime contractor to Navair.

Navair also funded a 1975 study on the engine carried out jointly by Rolls and PWA. There were four alternatives: the Pegasus 104, which compared with the AV-8A engine features aluminium casings, strengthened gearbox and drive, and various life-improvement changes; the Mk 104 with small changes to improve maintainability and give a TBO (time between overhauls) of 1,000 hours; the Pegasus 11D with small aerodynamic changes giving 800lb more thrust; and an 11D with the 1,000-hour life. Not submitted was the Pegasus 11+ with slightly raised TET (turbine entry temperature) giving thrust raised from 21,500 to 22,500lb. The final chapter outlines the engine situation today, which has by no means stood still at Bristol; but the US choice in early 1976 was the second one above, with improved maintainability only and intense concentration on reducing total life-cycle costs.

Virtually all the changes in the AV-8B took place on the airframe, including the nozzles. Together they add up to a complete transformation of the aircraft, and one can feel nothing but admiration for the St Louis engineers who accomplished this in 1975. They had the advantage of outstanding facilities, including those of the Navy and NASA, and in particular of a completely developed national technology in the application of carbon-fibre composites to primary airframe structure. This was the most glaring example of how much faster carbon and graphite composites have been developed for primary structure in the USA than in Britain, despite the fact that modern carbon/graphite fibres pyrolized from PAN precursor material had been originally developed in 1964-66 at Farnborough, England. Though Britain had carried out many research projects and acquired experience of carbon and graphite composites in such structures as airline passenger floors and access panels, the important stage of clearing advanced composites for primary structure has taken years longer than it should. Even in 1984 Britain has yet to create a

MARINES
158394
MARINES
AV-8B

MARINES
McDONNELL
DOUGLAS

2
MARINES
AV-8B
703
04

structure similar to the AV-8B wing or tailplane which were designed in 1975.

Aerodynamically the wing is based on the final standard of AV-16A subsonic wing, though with refinements. Totally unlike that of the Harrier, it has a deep supercritical section, with thickness of 11.5% at the root and 7.5% at the tip. Instead of being clearly a swept wing it is more accurately one tapered on the leading edge; compared with the Harrier the span and area are increased by 20% and 14% respectively. The main wing box is entirely of graphite/epoxy composite, and the degree of redundancy is shown by the fact that it has eight spars, each with a sine-wave web. It forms an integral tank which, together with a small additional volume resulting from the reprofiled engine inlets, adds a remarkable 50% to the internal fuel capacity.

For ease of repair, mechanical fastenings are used in preference to bonding. The skins are one-piece, and the upper skin is removable for inspection. Three stores stations are provided under each wing, supported by ribs of forged titanium, and the leading edge is light alloy. The trailing edge is totally new. The outrigger gears are moved inboard to reduce track from 22 to 17 feet, improving deck and road manoeuvring, and the leg fairings are replaced by doors. Outboard are large graphite/epoxy ailerons terminating well inboard from the tips and arranged to droop in the STO mode. Inboard of the outriggers are the flaps, and these are perhaps the most important new feature. In the Harrier the circulation round the wing is adversely affected by the powerful pumping effect of the engine nozzles, especially the front pair, which induces a mild reverse circulation in the STO mode which reduces net lift. MCAir and NASA sought to re-arrange the wing, flaps and nozzles to achieve the optimum positive circulation.

This was eventually accomplished by extending the front nozzles to a zero-scarf (end cut off at 90°) form essentially like rectangular-section pipes, and adding extremely broad flaps hinged to long brackets well below the wing. As the nozzles rotate in the STO mode the flaps depress to just over 61°, while large flap slot doors preserve the upper surface profile. The rear nozzles induce a powerful circulation over the flaps in much the same way as traditional blown flaps or the USB (upper-surface blowing) of the YC-14 transport. Tests with a 1/15 model and then the full-scale aircraft, in the giant 40 by 80 foot NASA Ames tunnel confirmed an increase in STO lift of more than 6,700lb.

Again totally new, the tailplane (horizontal stabilizer) is a masterpiece of simple design by MCAir. It comprises an aluminium leading edge, graphite/epoxy (GE) lower skin with integral GE woven-cloth spars, GE upper skin, composite trailing edge detachable in the field, and an aluminium-alloy centre piece in the fuselage riding on the pivots and driven by the surface power unit. Larger than the Harrier tailplane and of cropped delta shape, the structure eliminates previous problems of ground damage and honeycomb delamination.

The third large area of black carbon is the forward fuselage. Taking a leaf from the Sea Harrier book, the cockpit has been raised about 10.5 inches, the canopy raised and redesigned (but unrelated to that of the Sea Harrier) and the structure assembled from integrally stiffened left and right sandwich skins with a bolted floor and bulkheads. In the initial radarless AV-8B the nosecone is detachable for access to avionics.

To balance the new nose the rear fuselage is extended 18 inches and the fin increased in height. Originally the Sea Harrier fin was adopted, but a production 8B would have a redesigned fin with similar area, reduced height and weight and fewer parts. British Aerospace Kingston/Brough Division retains responsibility for the vertical tail and rear fuselage, the latter being stiffened by new side panels.

Weight-saving has been as remarkable as the increments in added lift, as shown in an accompanying diagram. Some 50 lb might later be saved by making the new engine nozzles of titanium, and their lift in VTO/STO is increased by boxing in the region into which they discharge by the deep inboard pylons. Another lift increment results from the new inlet system, which, though smaller than that of the AV-16A, has a cross-section matched to the modest predicted increases in thrust, throat area being increased from 9.2 to 9.7 sq ft, for example. The lip is no longer a circular arc but a 2:1 ellipse, and the auxiliary suck-in inlet doors have been increased in area in AV-16A style to a double row of 8.4 sq ft, an increase of 133%. At the same time the basic inlet is matched to high-altitude cruise airflow and reduces drag by eliminating spillage.

From the start of P.1127 work the interaction between the jets and the aircraft had been recognised to be complex and central to the entire performance in the VTO mode, particularly when on or near the ground. Part of the interaction may be advantageous, the jets feeding a high-pressure cushion under the aircraft. More often the results are adverse. The jets supply a cushion all right, but the air and hot gas escapes by flowing at high speed round the lower fuselage, the high speed meaning low pressure. The fuselage is literally sucked down against the ground, in effect greatly increasing the weight. Moreover, ingestion of the hot gas by the engine causes sharp rises in inlet temperature and flow distortion, resulting in severe and often rapidly varying reduction in engine thrust and surge margins.

Top: The No 2 YAV-8B, seen here with AIM-9L Sidewinders and seven Snakeyes, was lost on its 106th flight on 15 November 1979. It had an engine problem, and the engine flamed out and refused to relight whilst the aircraft was being ferried to St Louis. An RAF evaluation team accordingly had to wait./*MCAir*

Above left: This is the part of the AV-8B built by British Aerospace, and a very advanced and refined rear fuselage it is. This was the first to be delivered to production standard, for static testing at St Louis in spring 1981. Numerically controlled machining reduces the number of parts and the potential leak paths in integral tankage, and the ratio of strength to weight is significantly higher than for earlier Harriers. /*BAe*

Above: Not only does the AV-8B have 1½ times the internal fuel capacity of previous Harriers but it can ferry with four 300 US gallon drop tanks, giving a range of around 2,900 miles; February 1981 picture./*BAe*

By the early 1970s both Hawker and MCAir were paying more attention to ways of increasing the net lift force as an obvious route to greater loads of weapons or fuel. The St Louis team quickly realized that the concept of strakes in lieu of gun pods could be taken much further, and by early 1976 were testing various LIDs (lift-improvement devices) which sought to box in the region of the belly where the fountains (the jets rising after reflection from the ground) strike the aircraft. The final arrangement was a pair of strakes added along the underside of the gun pods and a hinged 'dam' retracted and lowered hydraulically in sequence with the landing gear to close the space between the pods at the upstream end. The dam assists in trapping the high-velocity fountains and also reduces reingestion, typically resulting in inlet temperatures 20°C lower. The first complete LID/dam set was tested on an AV-8A and showed the remarkable gain of 1,220 lb in VTO lift when tested full-scale at NASA Ames. When tested on a YAV-8B it was found that these improvements also eliminate cobblestone buffet on the underside of the aircraft and give so much extra lift that in a vertical landing the aircraft sinks to a height of about 20 feet and then refuses to descend further until the throttle is slightly closed.

With a virtual desert in engine funding the AV-8B powerplant was accepted as the F402-RR-406, almost identical to the Sea Harrier's Mk 104 but with additional detail changes to enhance life and meet severe requirements for maintainability. It drives a 20 kVA IDG (integrated-drive generator) supplying an electrical system with many new features including nickel/cadmium batteries. Other systems incorporate on-board oxygen generation, Dunlop carbon brakes and Sea Harrier type cast aluminium wheels, Sea

Harrier environmental control and a removable/retractable inflight-refuelling probe.

Avionics are largely new. The nose is occupied by the Hughes ARBS (angle-rate bombing set) in which a dual-mode laser/TV tracker feeds target angle and angle rate to the weapon-delivery computer and HUD. Originally designed for the A-4M, the ARBS gives accurate day/night delivery of "iron bombs" as well as laser-guided munitions or the TV-steered Maverick. Not unnaturally many of the new avionics and cockpit interfaces are borrowed from the F/A-18, for which the AV-8B has had to fight for funds. Examples include the Hotas (hands on throttle and stick) controls for virtually all electronic and ordnance functions, AYK-14 mission computer, ASN-130 inertial navigation system and ASPJ (advanced self-protection jammer) carried on the centreline pylon and ECM-resistant fibre-optic looms for digital data. Tail RWR and rear-fuselage chaff/flare dispenser are similar to the AV-8C. Anyone used to the F/A-18 digital cockpit would be immediately at home in an AV-8B, and Smiths supply a related HUD.

Of course, the AV-8B was planned to fit into the Marines' overall effort without additional demands; indeed it was calculated by MCAir that maintenance burden could be reduced. Maintenance man-hours per flight hour were planned to be 16.9, compared with an achieved (1972-75 average) for the AV-8A of 21.7. Mean flight time between failures was planned to rise from 1.5 to 2.4 hours, while operational readiness was calculated to reach 75% compared with 50 (RAF squadrons average 75-80%). All this while carrying 50% more internal fuel and an ordnance load which on most mission profiles is more than double that of the AV-8A. The centreline point is rated at 1,000 lb, flanked by the gun pods; inboard pylons are each 2,000 lb, intermediates 1,000 lb and the new outboards 630 lb though usually occupied only by single AIM-9L Sidewinders. Total useful load for a rolling takeoff is 17,000 lb, of which 9,200 lb can be weapons and suspension hardware. From a 1,000 foot runway on a tropical day the 8B can lift 16 Mk 82 bombs weighing 9,120 lb and fly a low-level mission radius of 185 nautical miles (213 miles). It can even take a 7,000 lb load from a vertical takeoff, while as a contrast ferry range with four 300 US gal (250 gal) drop tanks exceeds 2,850 miles.

Most of these figures were known with some assurance as early as 1975 as the result of tunnel-testing at NASA Ames of a full-scale AV-8B based on a crashed AV-8A, with a quickly modified wood/metal wing. It is fair to comment that when MCAir became involved with the Harrier the company had no idea so much could be done to increase its flight performance, to the point where the operational

Right: Manufacturer's three-view drawing of the production AV-8B, with gun pods but without pylons./*MCAir*

Below right: An unusual view of the first AV-8B development prototype (161396) hovering at St Louis in the hands of Charlie Plummer on its first flight on 5 November 1981./*MCAir*

value of each aircraft in Marine missions is multiplied approximately threefold. In March 1976 the DSARC (Defense Systems Acquisition Review Council) authorized a limited flight-test programme using two YAV-8B aircraft rebuilt from AV-8As (158394-5) with most of the more significant changes such as the new wing, LIDs and inlets, but retaining the old cockpit and systems. The first was ready 53 days ahead of schedule, and 188 lb under the calculated empty weight of 12,400 lb, so that it was only about 30 lb heavier than an AV-8A! Flying began at St Louis on 9 November 1978. Results generally confirmed prediction, and unexpectedly took in ski launches after the Marines bought an MGB ramp from Fairey and began trials in 1979 at 12°. The only significant trouble was drag caused by separation at the underside of the wing root, rectified by various changes.

By late 1979 the production wing had been finalised and tested, the new cockpit built and approved, and a limited move made towards FSD (full-scale development) with a $35 million award for long-lead items for four AV-8B production-type aircraft, the first to fly in October 1981 and each assigned to a major test programme. Sadly, in the face of any kind of common sense, the Carter administration from the outset regarded the entire programme as tainted by its foreign origin, and approached it in a negative manner. It has had to fight every inch of the way, largely because in a tight fiscal environment the gigantic escalation in costs of other Navy votes, such as the F/A-18 and all major ship programmes, has kept the AV-8B in the role of an expendable outsider. One posture, never before adopted for a major US weapon system, has been to make a go-ahead depend on foreign export sales. Both Dr Perry and Carter's SecDef himself, Harold Brown, made it clear they wanted to pour all the money into the F/A-18, as being a "more efficient" solution. When asked why just the AV-8B programme should be axed if no export customers emerged, Perry replied that it was "an inefficient project that consumes funds needed for overall force modernization". This black-is-white nonsense was not new to the Marines, but the three years of delaying tactics had by July 1980 added $920 million to the programme cost for the planned 336

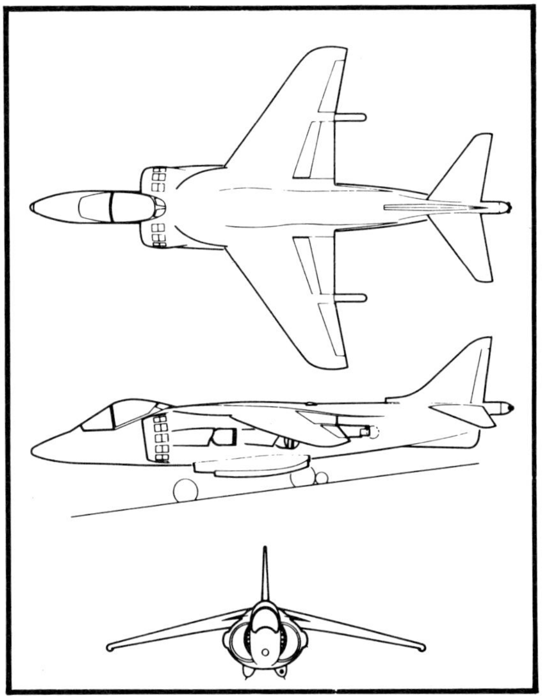

inventory aircraft, and this tragic and unnecessary waste of money and time can never be recovered. The F/A-18A is an excellent, if very expensive, aircraft, but it cannot operate unless it has a giant fully equipped carrier or a major land airbase. The one aircraft that offers the capability of versatile airpower with neither of those things is the AV-8B Harrier II, and it should never have been shunted to one side for purely political reasons.

Had the British government not so foolishly opted out in March 1975 the delay would never have occurred, and Harrier II would have been a 50/50 programme. As it is, the reluctance of the British government to come to any decision merely prolonged the agony until July 1981, when at last it was decided to ditch British Aerospace, take the easy way out by adopting what by this time had become an American product and leave the industrial partners to thrash out whatever percentage shares they could agree on. The British Defence Minister said 'Subject to the conclusion of satisfactory arrangements for collaboration. . . we envisage acquiring 60 AV-8Bs for the RAF'. The decision on proceeding with the programme was announced in Washington on 24 August 1981.

The initial announced requirement comprises 257 AV-8B Harrier II aircraft for the Marine Corps plus 60 Harrier GR5 for the RAF. The total programme comprises the two YAV-8B rebuilds, four FSD (full-scale development) aircraft, 12 pilot-production aircraft, 18 limited-production aircraft and 306 full-production aircraft. The last 336 are all for the Marine Corps inventory and will be substantially identical, but the different contracts specify slight variations in such things as tooling, vendor sources and techniques used in manufacture.

The AV-8B build standard continued to develop into early 1982. The final decision was to exclude radar and any internal ECM other than the Goodyear ALE-39 chaff/flare dispenser, the usual ECM pod being the ALQ-164 carried on the centreline. The gun selected is the General Electric GAU-12/U, carried in the left ventral strake/pod, with 300 rounds carried in the corresponding strake on the right. The Lerx (leading-edge root extension, described in the next chapter) is only 55% as large as the British Aerospace design, yet it still increases the instantaneous turn rate from 16° to 20° per second, meeting the RAF agility requirement. Other changes include the extended rear fuselage for increased internal equipment capacity (including ALE-39), a larger canopy giving improved all-round view in conjunction with a birdproof one-piece wrap-round windshield, and predominantly carbon-fibre construction for not only the wing but also the forward fuselage, tailplane and rudder. An extremely

Above: YAV-8B No 3 has no nose boom or inboard wing fences, but has the Lerx (leading-edge root extension) additions at the root of the wing. Note the large fin-like ventral strakes forming part of the LIDs (lift-improvement devices). In the production aircraft these are replaced by gun pods./*MCAir*

Left: The Harrier II cockpit is a generation newer than that of any Harrier I. This is an AV-8B; the GR.5 will have the right panel filled by a moving-map display. The HUD dominates the view ahead, with the UFC (up-front control) for CNI (com/nav/ident) below it. On the left is the MFD (multifunction display) on whose large square screen can be shown nav/mission plots, sensor pictures and many other things including very detailed radar warning information./*MCAir*

Above right: BuAer No 161397, the second YAV-8B, retained the nose boom but had the Lerx extensions from the start (these are much smaller than the original British pattern). It is shown in its colourful manufacturer's livery in April 1982./*MCAir*

Below right: First flown on 4 June 1982, the No 4 FSD aircraft is painted in low-visibility grey. It is seen here in the neighbourhood of NAS Patuxent River in October of that year./*MCAir*

Far right: Because of the great difference between the TAV-8A and the AV-8B the former cannot serve as a satisfactory conversion trainer, and McDonnell Douglas was asked to develop a dual-pilot TAV-8B. This is a provisional three-view./*MCAir*

welcome refinement is the provision of a bolt-on pack housing a fully retractable inflight-refuelling probe; this is attached in the top of the left inlet fairing.

Commercially the agreed deal is that on all US Harrier II procurement, taken at present to mean 340 Marine Corps aircraft including the four FSDs, the airframe work-split is MCAir 60% and British Aerospace 40%. Under MCAir general manager AV-8B Edwin A. Harper the programme is based at St Louis, with MCAir prime contractor responsible for assembly and flight test of the AV-8B Harrier II. BAe contributes the rear-centre and rear fuselage, fin, rudder, complete reaction control system and rear landing gear. For the RAF Harrier GR5 the prime contractor is BAe, and in this case with a 50/50 work-split on the airframe. For this aircraft BAe also supplies the Lerx, forward landing gear and tailplane, and carries out assembly and flight test. For third-party orders the split agreed is MCAir 75, BAe 25. On the engine, Pratt & Whitney has an agreement under the terms of which it will manufacture, and supply to Rolls-Royce, 25% by value of each engine for the USMC, or other US customer.

The four FSDs were ordered on 12 April 1979. These were the first aircraft that could properly be called Harrier IIs and all flew between 5 November 1981 and 4 June 1982. Two other airframes were built for static and fatigue testing, the latter demonstrating a 24,000-hour life by July 1982 to clear the aircraft to twice the stipulated figure of 6,000 hours. Hurdles cleared in 1982 included the stores-separation programme with nearly 58 tons of diverse weapons released in 103 flights, the electromagnetic compatibility testing, engine-propulsion and missile-firing trials, the Navy Preliminary Examination (with good marks) and the world's first hands-off automatic VL using the production Sperry autopilot, which uses new computer contol laws to provide perfect three-axis control at zero airspeed.

Full production at St Louis began in 1983, the first 12 being the pilot-production batch for BIS trials and delivery from October 1983 to MCAS Cherry Point in the pilot-conversion role. Initial operational capability is due in mid-1985, and at a delivery rate of $4\frac{1}{2}$ aircraft per month the St Louis line will take until 1989 to re-equip the three AV-8A squadrons plus five A-4 Skyhawk units. From the same line will come 12 aircraft for the Spanish Arma Aérea to supplement

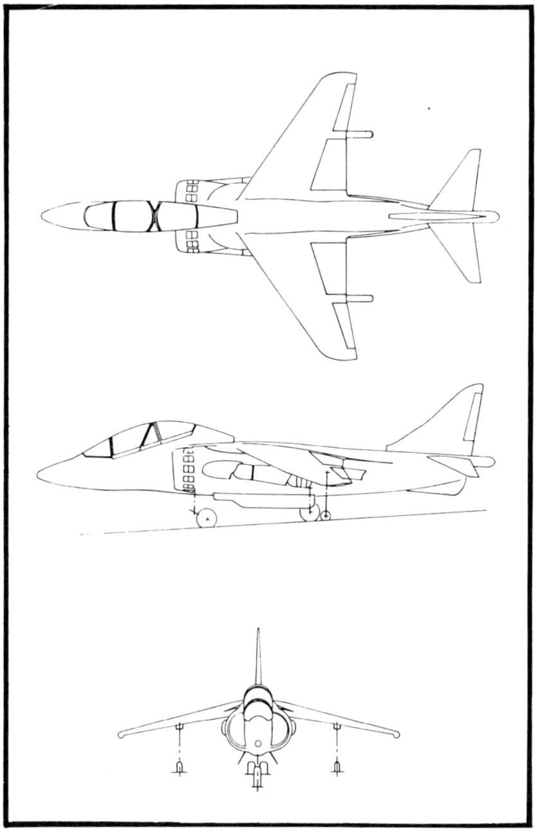

Above left: A model of the TAV-8B showing the great difference in height between the two cockpits. Despite the existence of the British Aerospace two-seater it will be a completely fresh design./*MCAir*

Below left: The No 3 aircraft had handled many ordnance carriage and release tests, mainly from Patuxent River. Here a bomb load of 9,120lb is demonstrated, 16 Mk 82 bombs each weighing 570lb. /*MCAir*

Below: A view of the first AV-8B Harrier II to enter service with the US Marine Corps at Cherry Point, NC./*MCAir*

Right: Comparative views of the first two installations of the American gun adopted for the AV-8B, in which the General Electric GAU-12/U is housed in the left pod while the 300 rounds of 25mm ammunition (more than twice the bulk of 20mm) fills the right pod. The initial installation was in YAV-8B No 158394; orbiting over the Pax runway is grey-painted FSD No 4 in April 1983./*MCAir*

and then replace the AE-1 Matadors from 1987; the Spanish contract price announced in August 1982 was $379 million including spares and support.

RAF Harrier GR5s are being produced to a later timetable. They will be preceded by two FSD aircraft to clear the aircraft to a more severe fatigue spectrum matched to sustained low-level operations in Germany, and to fly the special trials needed for RAF weapons which include the two gun pods containing the new Aden 25mm cannon. The GR5 has many detail differences, the most externally evident being a different RWR system and two additional stores (Sidewinder) pylons in line with the outrigger gears. Production deliveries to the RAF are due to begin in 1986.

To support the AV-8B training requirement the USMC expects to need a further 18 two-seaters, and as the TAV-8A is no longer representative MCAir has proposed a completely new dual-control version of the Harrier II designated TAV-8B. The forward fuselage will be new, with deeply stepped cockpits under a new canopy unlike that of the RAF T4, and the taller vertical tail will also be new. TAV-8B manufacture was to begin in 1983 for a first flight in 1985. TAV-8B operations would begin in 1986 at MCAS Cherry Point, passing out 120 Harrier II pilots annually.

9
In the South Atlantic

On Friday 2 April 1982 Argentine sea, air and land forces invaded the Falkland Islands. On the same day the British Prime Minister announced the formation of a Task Force to recover the islands, should all diplomatic efforts to obtain a settlement fail.

Thus, in a theatre as remote from Europe as it is possible to imagine, the stage was set for an unexpected and unwanted war which will provide material for analysis for years to come. It resulted in a response by the British armed forces and manufacturing industry that was greater and very much faster than most observers would have deemed possible. It saw sea-skimming anti-ship missiles used for the first time; paradoxically Britain's Sea Skua, which in seven shots performed flawlessly, is unknown to the world's public, whereas France's Exocet gained fantastic worldwide fame despite the generally agreed consensus that both the missiles which struck British warships failed to explode.

In almost every way much more significant than the sea-skimming missile, the other new weapon blooded in the South Atlantic in 1982 was that described in this book. Before this war there were perhaps still more military leaders around the world either disinterested in jet V/STOL or simply unprepared to consider it objectively than those who could see that in any future war it might be the only kind of airpower that could survive. But to retake the Falklands there was no possible alternative: the Harrier was the only airpower possible.

Even today there are a few students of war who have the vague idea that Britain was reluctantly forced to use Sea Harriers and Harriers because it had no large carriers able to operate conventional fixed-wing aircraft: in other words that jet V/STOL was a kind of second-best. Those who were there are left in no doubt that, even had the Royal Navy possessed all the giant carriers of the US Navy, for most of the time that fighting was in progress these ships would have been unable to operate. Even if conventional aircraft had managed to be shot off the bows, they would have been unable to recover in blizzard conditions with 100ft cloudbase and horizontal visibility down to 200ft, with decks heaving 30-40ft vertically and winds gusting to 60kts.

Gales and ice did make one Sea Harrier slide off the deck into the sea, and two others simply vanished into a blizzard and were never seen again (and are presumed to have collided or flown into the sea). Against this can be set the deployment of airpower 8,000 miles from home which, though heavily outnumbered, set an air combat record that has never been equalled in actual war (because the ratio was infinite) in 2,000 combat missions that devastated ground targets defended by massed batteries of triple-A and SAMs and struck such fear into the courageous Argentinian pilots that the Sea Harrier was quickly named 'Black Death'.

On 2 April 1982 none of this could be predicted. All that was certain was that the Sea Harrier was the only aircraft that could serve as fixed-wing airpower to fly all the missions needed in a modern war: interception (CAP and deck alert), strike (loft bombing, medium level bombing and dive attack), ground attack (at low level, using bombs, smart weapons, rockets and cannon), reconnaissance (using various sensors over sea and land) and radar suppression. It was thus a one-type air force. Just as there were no alternates (navigational diversions) available to aircraft making the almost 4,000-mile flight south from Ascension Island to the Falklands, so there were no alternatives to the unique Royal Navy 'jump jet'.

The only alternative, in fact, was the same aircraft only different. Because so few Sea Harriers had been ordered, and because attrition in combat might reduce their numbers by half in a few days, it was decided to back up this puny force with some RAF Harrier GR3s. By 1982 the Harrier had been in front-line service 13 years. Its pilots were vastly experienced in day close-support missions, including reconnaissance, and had operated from harsh cleared sites from Norway to Belize. Most had never even seen any kind of aircraft carrier, never had air-to-air weapons or pretensions, and were usually not night-

Above right: Severe electromagnetic interference aboard ships forced the RAF to switch to the RN rocket pod, firing 36 rockets of 2in calibre. Here GR.3 XW767 flies clearance trials on 23 April 1982./*RAF Wittering*

Right: XW767 also flew clearance trials for AIM-9B Sidewinders, at that time available only on a single installation as had previously been flown at Boscombe (see page 42). /*RAF Wittering*

COLES

qualified. In contrast the Sea Harrier had been in service a mere three years and the aircraft were all virtually new. Pilots frequently had a mere 15 hours on type (though a major role was played by very experienced RAF pilots on exchange duties) and the Sea Harrier is configured and tasked very much in the air-to-air mission, operating from a heaving deck by day or night and in impossible weather. Significantly, 52° south latitude is rather a long way from fixed-wing anti-submarine and ocean-patrol aircraft, home-based tankers and, not least, from high-flying airborne early-warning radar surveillance aircraft. British industry did a few marvels in the spring of 1982 but a Pegasus-powered V/STOL radar station is a non-starter. And the eminently sensible early-warning version of the Sea King helicopter had consistently been refused funding, as an economy measure.

It was also an economy measure that had deleted from the procurement machine at least one batch of 10 Sea Harriers. Thus in April 1982 there were 34 of these vital aircraft on order, of which 33 had been delivered (the last, ZA195, was incomplete). Of the 33, one had crashed in Cornwall (XZ454) and another was lost at Yeovilton during the conflict (XZ438), while XZ440 was on trials at Boscombe and was not transferred to naval charge. On the morning of 2 April there were five assigned to 800 Sqn aboard *Hermes* and five to 801 aboard *Invincible*. By 4pm on the same day both ships were getting ready to sail, having had their air units greatly augmented by aircraft and personnel from other squadrons, notably from 899 HQ Sqn at Yeovilton. *Hermes* sailed with 12 Sea Harriers and *Invincible* with 10.

Combined with greatly increased quantities of helicopters, stores and equipment, this made the flight decks overcrowded, but as soon as the Task Force cleared the English Channel intensive working-up began to transform two squadrons with many extremely inexperienced pilots, many of whom had not even previously met, into the most mature and combat-capable units possible. All embarked Sea Harriers were hand-painted extra dark sea grey over

Above left: No 1 Sqn did a quick conversion course on RNAS Yeovilton's ski ramp from 14 April 1982 (the same day the unit was advised of its assignment to Operation Corporate). Each pilot fitted his single practice 'jump' in between the urgent aircraft mods. This is XW765./*Fleet Air Arm (Phot)*

Left: In the last week of April BAe designed and installed a fitting of the same I-band transponder as carried by the Sea Harrier, for instant positive identification on ship radars. It resulted in a bulge under the laser nose./*HMS Hermes*

the undersurfaces, matching the sides and top, and the national insignia were hand-painted as B-type (red/blue only) for reduced contrast. Individual aircraft numbers were reduced to a two-digit code painted in black instead of white.

Trials at Yeovilton and Boscombe included DACT (dissimilar air-combat training) against French Mirages and Super Etendards, fitting and clearing of the BL.755 cluster bomb and newly issued AIM-9L 'all-aspect' version of Sidewinder, new software for the weapon-aiming subroutines to allow loft bombing from an offset (radar) IP (initial point, a clearly visible landmark not too far from the target) in the attack role, and clearance for ski takeoff at a new overload weight with two 300gal (1500litre) drop tanks for ferry purposes. Every combat mission was flown with 100gal tanks and guns.

Throughout the campaign the standard launch was a rolling takeoff over the ski-jump (7° on *Invincible*, 12° on *Hermes*) not necessarily with the ship steaming into wind. As the force continued south from Ascension the weather became worse, the decks being perpetually wet and eventually covered with ice. Width of the available runway was 45ft (14m), and for a stream departure aircraft were marshalled in a row at 100ft (30m) intervals, launches being spaced 15 seconds apart. On combat missions aircraft were tasked in pairs, and it became routine to assign aircraft and pilots on a basis of operational need, so each aircraft was flown by many pilots (at the outset there were 1.2 pilots per aircraft, rising later to 1.4). South of Ascension strict radio silence was preserved, and there was no possibility of diversion to any land.

While the ships moved in close battle stations, maintaining ceaseless ASW and air surveillance, the weather deteriorated until visibility was typically between 0.5 mile and 200ft, dropping to zero in snow blizzards, with cloud base between 100 and 200ft (30-60m). Seas were invariably heavy, flight decks moving vertically through 30ft (9m). Although aircraft recovered to the decks from all directions, with any kind of WOD (wind over deck) speed and direction, all landings were vertical, burning only a few hundred pounds of fuel between the high-speed approach towards the ship's image on the Blue Fox radar display and the aircraft being parked and shut down.

Recoveries took place routinely in weather that would have halted flying from conventional carriers. In the poorest visibility the ships occasionally dropped spaced flares astern, but the standard recovery relied on the aircraft's own radar and internal approach aid. After the decelerating transition to jetborne flight off the port (left) side of the ship the routine was to hold station for a few seconds whilst selecting any clear patch of deck 60ft across. The aircraft would then transition inboard and make a VL (vertical landing), if necessary then taxiing forwards as instructed by deck marshals. On many occasions aircraft recovered with asymmetric stores. There was only a slight incident during well over 2,000 Harrier recoveries, and this was when the aircraft, with BL.755s still on board, made an untidy recovery to a deck that was pitching and rolling in a heavy sea and landed with its left outrigger hanging over the catwalk. The aircraft promptly tipped over on to its left-side BL.755, the right outrigger being high off the deck. Sheer manpower was used to pull the aircraft upright and roll it forward until the left outrigger was firmly on deck. The unserviceable BL.755 was tossed overboard, while the *serviceable* aircraft was readied for its next sortie.

How many other carrier-based aircraft could so easily shrug off an arrival with one wheel in the catwalk? Not only did the Falklands campaign abundantly establish powered-lift VL as the easiest, safest and most flexible type of recovery for any combat aircraft – ship or shore-based – but it enabled flying to continue in weather that would have halted operations by every other kind of jet combat aircraft.

Combat missions opened on Saturday, 1 May, with attacks on Stanley airport (in the wake of the first Vulcan bombing) and Goose Green. Ground fire was intense, though no SAMs were noted. One aircraft took a 20mm shell through the fin, which was given a patch repair, and the profusion of small-calibre strikes were routinely covered with Speed-tape (thin aluminium tape backed with adhesive). Most aircraft carried three 1,000lb bombs or three BL.755s, but a few had a centreline store and two Sidewinders and served also as escorts. Later on the same day aircraft scrambled to intercept Argentine Mirages and Canberras, all of which turned back before the Sea Harriers reached them. The only casualty was an Argentine Mirage shot down by ground fire in the first of several 'own goals'.

How the Sea Harrier would perform in air-to-air engagement was still a matter for conjecture, though it had had plenty of exposure to the F-5E, F-15 and F-16. In subsequent air operations over the islands there was generally, for various reasons, little warning of Argentine air attacks, so Sea Harriers flew standing patrols at medium altitude at selected points off West Falkland. Argentine aircraft typically had to fly 450-480 miles in each direction, but the larger forces of A-4 Skyhawks all had FR probes and the navy Super Etendards carried 'buddy' FR packs. Many had sufficient fuel for repeated attacking passes, though the Mirage and Dagger afterburners were so much dead weight if recovery at base was to be certain. In general, fuel states were not critical, and it is a reflection on the Sea Harrier that no Argentine pilot ever chose to stay and fight.

The first time Sea Harriers were able to intercept Argentine aircraft was on the evening of 2 May. Two aircraft of 801 on CAP were advised of incoming aircraft at high altitude. They were vectored towards them, climbing, and Flt Lt Paul Barton – one of seven RAF pilots with 800/801 – got them on his radar at a distance of just under 20 miles. They were Mirages, and the initial meeting was head-on, but Barton worked round to split them apart. They ignored him so he soon got on the tail of one and at about 800yd (2,400ft) fired a brief burst from his guns. Then he released a Sidewinder; the target aircraft instantly fireballed. This was to become typical. Though a final total of at least seven aircraft were to fall to the Sea Harrier's guns, the main air-to-air weapon was the

Left: Another of the weapons which RAF Harriers had never previously had was the Mk 13/18 Paveway II laser-guided bomb, based on the British thousand-pounder. Beyond is another 1 Sqn aircraft with BL.755 cluster bombs, one of the very few weapons the Treasury had actually permitted prior to April 1982. The Sea Harriers sharing *Hermes'* deck are 809, the scratch unit most of whose aircraft had to have GR.3 pylons./*HMS Hermes*

Right: This picture, at sunset on a rare fine day, shows the outline of the I-band chin transponder and its associated blade aerial, on a GR.3 of No 1 (F) Sqn./*HMS Hermes*

AIM-9L, and it established a remarkable record of 18½ kills in 24 firings. This figure of 77% contrasts with figures of around 20% for earlier versions in Vietnam (a few AIM-9G and -9H were also carried, but the 9L was involved in all live firings).

The first loss occurred on 4 May when XZ450, the first Sea Harrier ever to fly, was shot down over Goose Green. The pilot, Lt Cdr Nick Taylor of 800 Sqn, was killed. There is little doubt the aircraft was hit by a burst from 30 or 35mm AAA, one round exploding the integral tank in the left wing. Not much can be done to provide protection aginst visually sighted AAA, but it is nevertheless outrageous, in view of the basic missions for which all kinds of Harrier were designed, that there should have been no provision for any ECM installation. An internal chaff/flare dispenser had been planned from the start but funding had never been made available. As a temporary makeshift answer bundles of chaff were sandwiched between air/ground stores and the Sea Harrier's three available NATO-standard ERUs (ejector release unts) so that on release of the weapon the chaff was allowed to bloom. Later further bundles were jammed under the airbrake, and released on the pilot selecting a touch of airbrake – not enough significantly to slow the aircraft. There's nothing like a war for breaking a funding deadlock, and before the end of the fighting supplies of the Goodyear ALE-39 chaff/flare dispenser were with the Task Force (the same dispenser is used on USMC Harrier Is and IIs).

From the first discussion of the situation on 2 April one thing had been self-evident. All British airpower would be heavily outnumbered – Argentinian Mirage/Dagger forces alone outnumbered Sea Harriers two to one, and so did the A-4s – and unless something extraordinary was achieved in air combat the situation could only get worse, because 10 Argentinian losses would make little difference whereas 10 Sea Harriers lost would reduce the British force by half. So something had to be done to provide reinforcements, and the simplest thing was to cobble together a third squadron of Sea Harriers, using all remaining machines except two to maintain essential training at Yeovilton and XZ440 on special trials at Boscombe. The aircraft of the new squadron, eight in all, were professionally painted in a new low-visibility scheme of light grey overall, the undersides actually being in an even paler shade called Barley grey, with Type B roundels on each side of the nose below the grey finally appearing pale blue-grey and pink. Pilots quickly worked up at Yeovilton, but the unit was not ready to sail with the planned transport, *Atlantic Conveyor.* This container ship had been hastily converted to carry helicopters, Harrier spares and many other items, and a row of containers was arranged along each side of the deck to provide some protection to the space between. On 30 April the new squadron flew out from the UK to join the ship which had left a week earlier. Tankered by Victors, they set a new distance/endurance record for Harriers by

flying 9¼ hours non-stop to Ascension, from where they flew to make VLs aboard the container ship, where each was quickly wrapped in a Driclad cocoon, except for one aircraft held at readiness on the ship's pad.

The decision was also taken to deploy an RAF squadron of Harrier GR3s to make good Sea Harrier losses in the air-defence mission. No other shore-based aircraft in the world could so effortlessly have made the switch from land-based operations to the toughest imaginable combat missions from ships. The aircraft chosen were No 1 Sqn from Wittering, and the immediate task was to wire them for Sidewinders, the AIM-9B firing trials programme from Llanbedr/Aberporth being completed on 3 May. Before that time the aircraft, 14 in all, were given a radar transponder to enhance signature on carrier radars (resulting in an under-nose bulge), and extra drain plugs. Further trials were flown to clear the GR3 to fire the RN 2in (50.8mm) rocket from a 36-tube launcher instead of the 18-barrel 68mm SNEB pod, and also the Mk 13/18 Paveway II laser-guided bomb. No 1's pilots, very experienced in other ways, knew nothing about ship operations. For a start, on 14 April each did a crash course in ski-jumping at Yeovilton. Three jumps each had been planned but one was enough – the general view was 'there's nothing to it'.

On 3 May the first nine GR3s flew to RAF St Mawgan, Cornwall, and then with Victor support over the 4,260 miles to Ascension. Three remained there as air defence; the other six made a short hop aboard *Atlantic Conveyor,* which took them to 52°S. Reaching the task force on 18 May the reinforcing Harriers and Sea Harriers were quickly readied for flight. Their pilots took off on that day and the next from the small pad behind the foremast and flew across to *Hermes* (two Sea Harriers went to *Invincible)* to make VL arrivals. The RAF pilots had never seen a carrier before.

Subsequently the three on duty at Ascension, plus

Below: The detachment of 20 servicing tradesmen from RAF No 1 Sqn had to call on help from the RN for the one engine change needed. At least there was no snow and ice inside *Hermes'* hangar. Note Sea Harriers, Lynx and stack of Sea King blades./*HMS Hermes*

Right: Each combat sortie recovered by crabbing across from port (the left) to a position above a deck spot, synchronizing speed with the ship and then letting down vertically. Note: the fact all the photos were taken aboard one carrier does not mean we can forget about HMS *Invincible*!/*HMS Hermes via BAe*

Below right: A Sea Harrier of 800 Sqn recovers aboard *Hermes* with its AIM-9L Sidewinders unfired. These missiles, produced by a NATO group in Europe under US licence, proved devastating./*BAe*

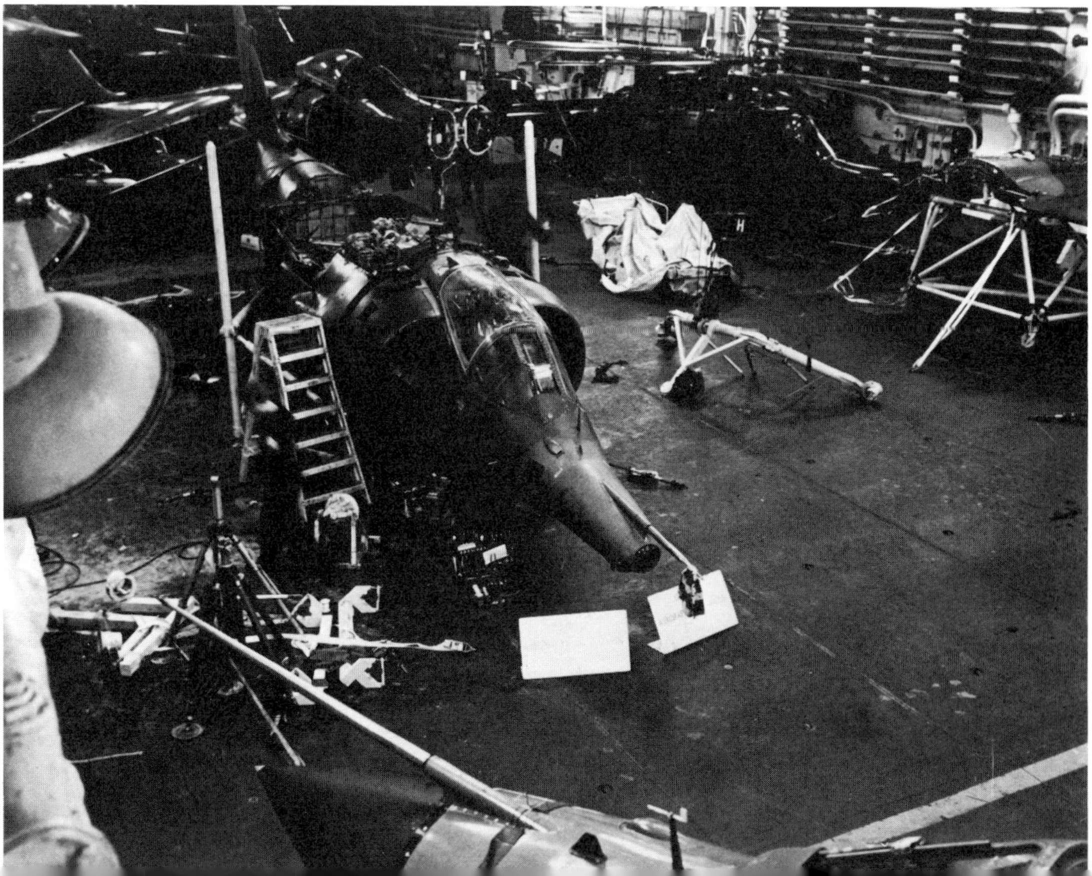

Above: The only obviously visible weapons on HMS *Broadsword* are the white sextuple launchers for BAe Dynamics Seawolf, providing vital point defence for *Hermes.* The Sea Harriers can be identified as from 800 (left) and 809, respectively./*BAe*

Left: Positioning an aircraft of 809 ready for a combat sortie, with a pair of 899 in the foreground. The Lynx is armed with Sea Skuas; three helicopters flew 3,043 combat hours, with virtually no malfunction, though three were lost on stricken ships./*BAe*

Right: The two types of British Harrier worked closely together during the 75 days of war. Operators here are RAF No 1 (F) Sqn and FAA 809 and 899 Sqns./*BAe*

a fourth, voyaged south aboard *Contender Bezant.* The final four flew non-stop to Ascension and then flew on to the carriers with the Task Force in a second 3,925-mile hop with no possibility of any alternates and total radio silence, finally to arrive for a VL on *Hermes* in the middle of an Argentine attack. The distance flown by these small single-seaters was similar to that from New York to New Zealand. Arrived aboard *Hermes*, probes were unbolted and in 30 minutes the final reinforcements were ready for action.

In fact, not a single Sea Harrier was lost in air combat, so instead of being whisked into CAP missions No 1 Sqn was instantly tasked with ground attack. The local naval commanders certainly had a point, because the nearly new Sea Harriers cost almost twice as much and were not only more versatile but irreplaceable, and while casualties were inevitable on attack missions there was a good chance that dogfights, as such, would never happen at all (they didn't). So from 19 May the dangerous low-level attack and recon was handled by the RAF, while the Sea Harriers handled the CAP to try to ward off the sustained Argentine air attacks.

The rest of the air war, as far as the Harriers were concerned, was basically one of remarkable success. Three GR3s were shot down, Flt Lt Bob Glover to a Blowpipe SAM at Fox Bay on 21 May, Sqd Ldr Bob Iveson to AAA over West Falkland on the 26th and Flt Lt Jerry Pook who was riddled by AAA and lost too much fuel to make it back to the ship. All pilots ejected, though Glover was for a time a prisoner of war. RAF Harrier operations were greatly assisted by Ferranti Ltd inventing and quickly delivering Finrae (Ferranti INertial Rapid ALignment Equipment) for quickly setting up the unchanged FE.541 inertial system on the heaving and oscillating deck. Unfortunately two Finraes were destroyed aboard *Atlantic Conveyor*, but the third was transferred to *Hermes*, the hastily debugged software program was sent down by satellite link, and No 1 Sqn was in business. After the first week all Sidewinder interfaces were removed, leaving the GR3s able to carry three heavy attack stores plus guns and tanks. Soon after the landing at San Carlos Royal Engineers constructed a shore base, using 1,200ft of MEXE strip, with dispersals at one end and standard pillow tanks for refuelling. Manned by a team of eight under a flight sergeant, this became a busy forward operating base to reduce dead time flying to the scene of action.

As for the Sea Harriers, the three squadrons continued their CAP, occasionally leavened by ground attack or anti-ship sorties, to gain a final score of 32 kills (18½ by AAM, 8½ with guns, 3 by cluster bombs and two from hitting the land or sea in combat). Just one more Sea Harrier was lost, an 801 Sqn aircraft flown by Flt Lt Ian Mortimer RAF, hit by

a Roland SAM off Stanley on 1 June. Mortimer spent the next nine hours in his dinghy.

Altogether Sea Harriers flew 1,893 combat sorties over the islands, 282 of them at night and almost all in extremely severe weather. Despite terrible working conditions on the exposed decks the aircraft availability was consistently above 80%, 800 Sqn seldom falling below 90% in over 1,000 missions and 801 reporting 'in excess of a staggering 99%' for the 600-odd missions tasked during the conflict phase of the campaign, Flying rate for the entire force throughout the 75 days averaged 55 hours per aircraft per month, in up to six sorties per aircraft per day. Pilots flew three or four missions a day, spending around 10 hours in the cockpit.

The extraordinary success of the Harrier and Sea Harrier surprised students of air warfare around the world, and caused a belated reappraisal of these aircraft among the world's air forces and navies, most of all in the Argentine whose pilots will confirm that the soubriquet 'Black Death' was not bestowed in any jocular mood. Some of the results are unlikely to read across to other wars. After the crazy initial meeting, in which Argentine pilots simply shot from the hip with Magics and Sidewinders, with no hits scored, there was nothing that could be called an air combat. There were a few entertaining diversions – as when a Sea Harrier seemingly endlessly chased three small T-34B armed trainers in and out of the clouds at low level above Stanley – but almost every air-to-air engagement was a stern chase at over 500kts at minimum altitude. Some targets offered perfect boresight launches, but the AIM-9L kill probability of 77% was not entirely unreal because many of the targets were pulling all the g they could muster to try to escape. Likewise, many of the kills with Aden guns were against violently manoeuvring and agile targets. The breakdown of Sea Harrier kills is: Mirage/Dagger 12, A-4 Skyhawk 5, Pucará 1, Canberra 1, C-130 1 and helicopters 3. To this total of 23 can be added a further three probables, plus 15 destroyed on the ground.

After the cease-fire on Monday 14 June various Harrier and Sea Harrier units remained to defend the islands until progressively relieved by Phantoms from 17 October, after restoration and lengthening of the runway. The MoD announced an order for a further 14 Sea Harriers to replace losses and sustain a third squadron. All Harriers and Sea Harriers are more effective than before Operation 'Corporate', as the recovery of the islands was named, and further overdue improvements, such as the chaff/flare dispenser, are being retrofitted. But the main conclusion, that is now evident even to those whose minds were previously closed, is that no other aircraft could have done the job.

Above left: Ten minutes away from a fantastic welcome at Portsmouth on return from Operation Corporate, with Sea Harriers of 899 neatly ranged; nearest is No 14, with silhouettes of two Mirages and a Pucará on the left side of the nose. Facing the camera is a pale grey aircraft of 809, which returned to the Falklands aboard the newly commissioned *Illustrious* on 2 August./*BAe*

Above: The trials Sea Harrier XZ440 was used to clear the urgent carriage of 190 gal tanks and twin Sidewinders. Here there are AIM-9Bs on the right (starboard) wing and two of the new 9Ls on the left./*BAe*

Right: IN601, the first Sea Harrier for the Indian Navy, was first flown by Dunsfold test pilot Heinz Frick on 6 August 1982. The badge on the tail is the leopard emblem of 300 Sqn, which will be embarked aboard INS *Vikrant*./*BAe*

Below: A 1978 close-up showing the LERX (leading-edge root extensions) flown on a standard Harrier and demonstrated to offer aerodynamic advantages./*BAe*

10 Future Prospects

A good place to begin this overview is February 1965 when the Harrier was permitted to be studied after cancellation of the 1154. The outlook of the British Air Staff tends to oscillate between violent polarization on particular topics, and in the 1960s the topic was low-level attack with conventional weapons. Aerial combat was hardly considered, so it was natural to design the Harrier with an extremely small wing. This is ideal for 590 knots at 200 feet and also minimizes structure weight; but it resulted in poor manoeuvrability even at medium altitudes, and the odd characteristic of being able to get to 50,000 feet in less than four minutes but with no power of manoeuvre worth mentioning. (Wing loading is actually only 65% as high as that of the F-104S, but at a pinch the latter can fly much faster for a few minutes, and thus pull more g, before running out of fuel.)

When the first Harrier replacement studies took place around 1970 the low attack mission still predominated, and the result was Air Staff Target 403 for a modern tactical aircraft to replace both Harrier and Jaguar. AST.403 has been dropped in favour of a search for a common European combat aircraft, plus a purely RAF requirement for a V/STOL to replace the Harrier. The latter, one of the few cases where Britain is the only one in step, resulted in ASR. (Air Staff Requirement, not a mere target) 409, and though many schemes were explored it was always pretty evident the answer had to be a Harrier derivative rather than a new design. And it seems blindingly obvious to me that the place to put the aircraft are dispersed sites where the terrain provides a natural ski-jump. If necessary this could be graded by a dozer and covered with wire mesh. There are many hundred of such sites in Germany or England.

By 1974, before ASR.409 was issued, the RAF had become much more interested in air combat, partly because of the anticipated Warsaw Pact deployment of a new fighter generation by the mid-1980s and partly because of the Marines' exploration of viffing and consequent emergence of the Harrier as a hitherto unsuspected potential air-combat fighter. Kingston schemed a simple modification for the existing GR.3 force involving viffing nozzles and wiring for Sidewinders on the outboard pylons, as well as a more extensive retrofit of overwing pylons, closely resembling those of the Jaguar International, to carry Sidewinders, Magics or 150-gal tanks and thus leaving the underwing pylons available for offensive stores. The overwing pylons got as far as being aerodynamically test-flown in balsa-wood in 1975 but, though the retrofit bill for the whole force would not have exceeded £0.6 million, nothing more was done, and even today RAF Harriers have virtually no air-to-air capability

Looking ahead to the post-1984 era the RAF saw the need for tactical aircraft able to carry a heavy bomb load yet penetrate defences equipped with agile modern fighters. ASR.409 therefore specified rates of turn at least as good as those of the most manoeuvrable existing fighters. Details are classified, but it has been said that MCAir offered a turn rate of 19°/s with a developed AV-8B and learned that this fell short of the requirement. At this time the American aircraft was also in severe maximum-speed trouble, and when these shortcomings were added to the emotional need to keep the Harrier a British programme, find a solution that could be retro-fitted to existing Harrier GR.3s and give the best overall results for Britain, coming in as a minor partner on the AV-8B seemed a poor answer – at least to British Aerospace. Kingston derided the AV-8B as "a bomb truck" – which it is, and a good one. Moreover, the 8B was never intended as a retrofit, and has a stronger rear fuselage and new tailplane. These minimise cruise drag and improve manoeuvrability by enabling the viffing envelope to be opened out to 460 knots indicated with the nozzles at full power in the 98.5° braking position; and, as noted earlier, the new tailplane is simpler and tougher than the original. But

Above right: Final form of the 'Mk 5' Big Wing Harrier, which according to the RAE would indeed have met all the numbers stipulated in ASR.409. Note the raised cockpit and separate rear-fuselage airbrake./*BAe*

Right: Close-up of the left PCB nozzle on the old Pegasus 2 at Shoeburyness in 1980. It is canted downward, so the nozzles toe-in in VTO./*Rolls-Royce*

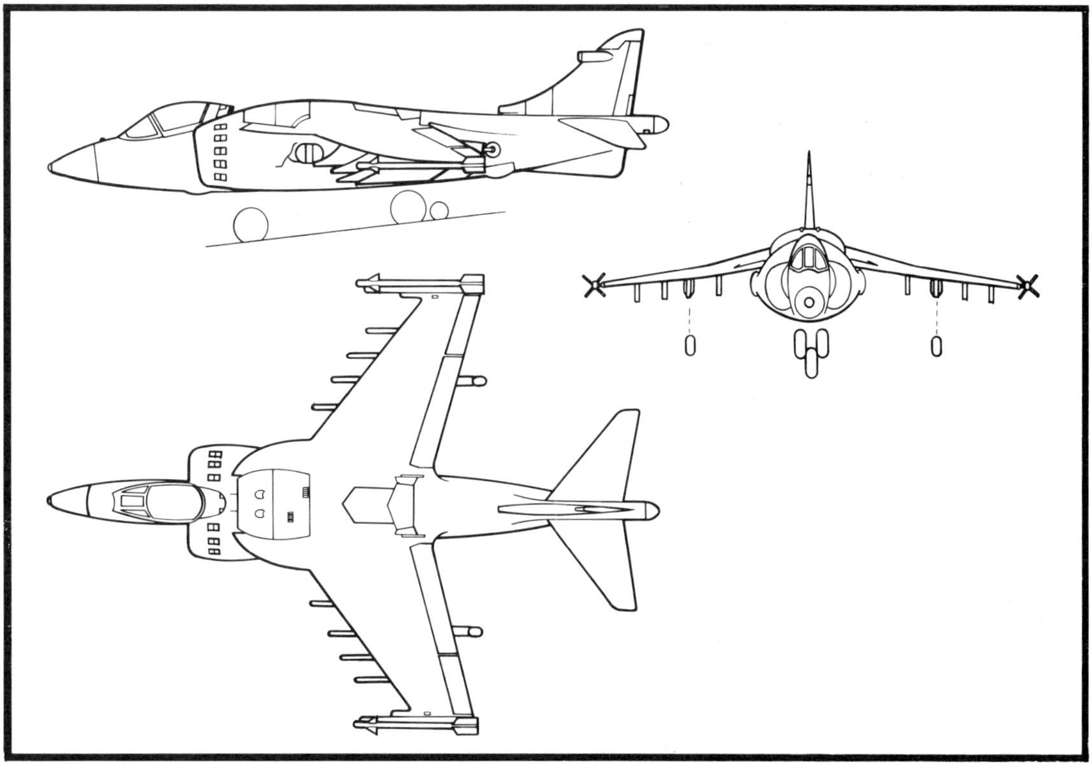

virtual inability of the AV-8B wing to be fitted to existing Harriers, except with rebuilding of the whole aircraft downstream, was a real problem. Throughout, at the political level, British Aerospace (as it became in 1977) naturally saw warning lights flashing at the idea of replacing the Harrier by the AV-8B. As was said at the 1980 Farnborough air-show, "Exporting the Harrier wasn't expected to go this far".

Nobody seems to have realized beforehand that the West's pioneer V/STOL, possibly the most important single type of combat aircraft, had become split down the middle. Those who created it had been prevented from building a new-generation Harrier to equal the improved version of the foreign partner; and so inevitably the happy relationship began to go sour. In Kingston's view the first thing to do was design a modern multi-role Harrier which could be created by modifying the GR.3; then this had to be adopted by the RAF instead of the 8B. To do this it was necessary to point out all the shortcomings in the American aircraft, as well as churn out piles of paper showing how much better off the UK would be in selling X all-British Advanced Harriers instead of a 45% share of Y AV-8Bs. This share comprises one-third of the airframe (10%), three-quarters of the engine (25%) and 10% by the UK equipment suppliers. Such things happen all the time in a free society, but they tend to strain friendships and waste time which, in an inflationary world, puts up the price alarmingly.

It was not difficult to show the MoD that a British "Big Wing" could be designed which would meet ASR.409 requirements, outperform some aspects of the AV-8B, and retrofit on existing Harriers. An MoD study contract was signed in 1978, as a result of which what has simply become known as the Big Wing was designed and tunnel-tested in model form; and two further add-ons, called Lerx (pronounced lurks) and Cads, were test-flown.

Lerx stands for leading-edge root extensions, and comprises curved-edge plates added ahead of the wing-roots with a function identical to the much longer LEX (pronounced as three letters) of the F-18 and the forebody strakes of the F-16. They not only add area but create strong rolling vortices at extreme angles of attack and thus delay separation and force the wing to continue to lift. When flown on XV277 later in 1978 they confirmed model tests in increasing maximum lift coefficient by 20% and enabling 0.5 to 1.0 g additional acceleration to be pulled for any given engine thrust. Naturally they degraded the already marginal longitudinal stability and could not be retrofitted by themselves, but were retained as a feature of the Big Wing. Cads (cushion-augmentation devices) are virtually the same as the LIDs of the AV-8B though the strakes have a leading edge at 90° to the airflow and the retractable dam is of different design. Cads were flown on XV277 at the same time as the Lerx, and performed as predicted.

Kingston designed the Big Wing from scratch. It has no kinship with the Harrier wing beyond sharing the same sweep angle on the trailing edge, and is also unrelated to the AV-8B wing, details of whose aerodynamics were classified by the US government despite the 1969 agreement between MCAir and Hawker for free exchange of information and the fact that the supercritical section was developed by NASA, a civilian agency. In any case a Kingston argument in favour of their wing is that it was based on newer technology; in a competitive situation such things tend to be overstated, but Kingston dated the AV-8B wing at 1974 and its own Big Wing at 1979

Compared with the American wing the Big Wing had greater span, greater area, smaller flaps and a less-extreme supercritical section, thickness/chord ratio being no less than 12.5% on the centreline and 9.2 at the tip, compared with 11.5/7.5. This enabled structure weight to be reduced, but unlike the graphite composite American wing the British structure would have been light alloy which made it heavier. Obviously it would have provided even more internal volume than the American wing, though internal fuel capacity was increased by only 245 gal compared with 316 for the AV-8B.

Fitting this wing to existing Harriers or Sea

Top right: This is what a PCB burner looks like. It is standing on its circular face mating with the vectoring nozzle; fuel pipes look silver. */Rolls-Royce*

Top, far right: For the 1990 era three-poster PCB V/STOL looks a dead certainty. This is one of the possible configurations, which could fly the missions of a Tornado or F-14 without needing a pretargeted airbase – and with unprecedented air-combat manoeuvrability. */Rolls-Royce*

Centre right: This model shows the extended fuselage, new wing and PCB front nozzles of the AV-8SX proposed jointly by McDonnell Douglas and Rolls-Royce.*/MCAir*

Right: This is how the 'three-poster' engine for future supersonic V/STOLs would be arranged. The front PCB nozzles are canted down (in this drawing they would not toe-in in VTO but be vertical) and the rear jetpipe is vectored by 180° rotation of the tapered section. */Rolls-Royce*

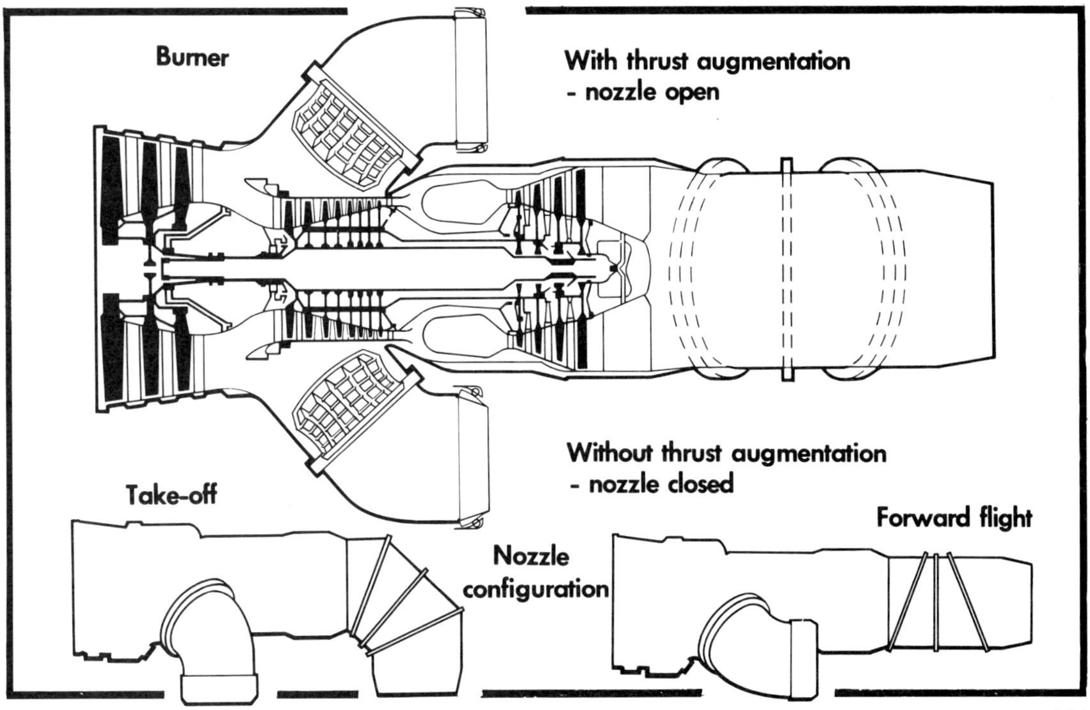
Burner
With thrust augmentation
- nozzle open
Without thrust augmentation
- nozzle closed
Take-off
Forward flight
Nozzle
configuration

Harriers would have been fairly straighforward, requiring only a fuselage hardpoint to carry the leading attachment of the Lerx and additional plumbing for the extra pylons, as well as modified root fairings and engine access doors. By mid-1979 the Air Staff had received detailed and priced BAe proposals for refitting the RAF Harriers, both with and without the two-seater. At the same time this proposal, which would have resulted in a Harrier GR.5 and possibly a T.6, was backed up by a brochure for a largely new aircraft known as the Super Harrier.

This would mate the new wing to a Sea Harrier forward fuselage, with or without Blue Fox radar but with a better nose profile than the GR.3, as well as the 11F-35 engine and enlarged and reprofiled inlets similar to those of the AV-8B, with double auxiliary doors. Ferranti digital INAS (inertial nav/attack system) would be fitted, and would be an easy retrofit on the GR.5. Thanks to a much-enhanced avionic kit the Super could be a much more versatile aircraft than the GR.5, though as the whole aircraft would be new it would cost at least twice as much.

While detailed investigation of the GR.5 and Super continued, the notion of re-winging the existing Harriers was dealt a severe blow by the statement in the 1980 Defence Estimates debate that 'The Big Wing is unlikely to be any part of an improvement programme of the GR.3' – which was taken to mean that there might be a GR.3 update but that it would not include the new wing.

The new US administration from 20 January 1981 certainly cleared the air and allowed the disgraceful time-wasting – which is reckoned to have added $1.3 billion to the AV-8B programme and £450 million to a UK buy of 60 Super Harriers – to come to an overdue end. In the United States the outgoing Carter administration signed into law the FY81 (Fiscal Year 1981) defence bill including not only $243 million for RDT&E (research, development, test and engineering) of the AV-8B but also $90 million for long-lead procurement of material for pilot production. But FY82 was devoid of production funds and contained only $231 million for yet further RDT&E.

As described in the AV-8B chapter the inevitable eventual decision was acceptance by Britain of the American product, but it would be wrong to regard this as a complete capitulation by Britain. Today's Harrier II represents a harmonious team effort by MCAir and BAe, in the planning and design phases as much as in manufacture. In many areas BAe's influence has been predominant, sometimes in a positive way and occasionally in exercising a restraining hand. For this reason the Harrier II has been an outstandingly successful machine, with large inputs from the F-15 and F/A-18 programmes in such challenging areas as the integration of the avionics, software, cockpit and weapons. The only significant hiccup was an initial shortfall in speed, and this was rectified by minor changes in body and wing root profiles. Undoubtedly the Harrier II represents the best that can be done today with the existing Pegasus engine.

But this is still only part of the adolescent process of the West's V/STOL. A fairly obvious next move is to go back to PCB and supersonics, so shortsightedly discontinued in 1965. Though air forces think it important, Mach 2 is of little value. It is seldom reached by any real squadron aircraft, and was never even approached in the 3 million combat hours by US aircraft in Vietnam. But something in excess of Mach 1 could be advantageous. So BAe, MCAir and Rolls-Royce have not been idle in studying future supersonic Harriers.

These would not use deep long-span wings like the Super or AV-8B, nor would they merely be warmed-over AV-16As. For one thing the basic four-poster engine would be replaced by a tripod, giving less drag and offering other improvements. As far back as 1971 RR Bristol was studying tripod Pegasus engines, one of which was selected for most of the supersonic AV-16S studies for around Mach 1.6. Beyond doubt, PCB is a must for supersonic V/STOLs, giving about 50% boost at takeoff, around 100% boost at Mach 1 and at least 150% at Mach 1.6 above 20,000 feet. And Mach numbers of the latter order are, for either prestige or for genuine operational reasons, demanded by the US Navy and Air Force in a whole spectrum of planned V/STOL missions for 1990 and beyond. There is no doubt that BAe and Rolls-Royce have a gigantic head start and could, with political leadership, create the next generation V/STOL family with supersonic performance.

A fumbling but welcome beginning of a mature V/STOL era took place in 1980 when an ancient Pegasus 2 went back into PCB testing at Shoeburyness. This rig soon demonstrated stable operation with distorted inlet flows, and the ability to cross-light via a small tube by extinguishing one PCB combustor using gigantic inflows of water and then relighting from the burner on the other side. The light-up and combustion characteristics at altitude were then explored at the National Gas Turbine Establishment, Pyestock, followed by reingestion and recirculation tests using the same engine in a crashed Harrier airframe slung from a crane. These tests will enable the optimum nozzle configuration to be investigated by 1985. With luck, by this time there should be at least one Mk 11F-35 engine running, as well as parts of a Mk 11-33 with PCB to be rated at 24,500 lb dry and 34,000 lb with PCB. Testing at the

RR Halford Lab at Hatfield has confirmed the performance of the new fan. By 1990 Rolls-Royce could deliver production examples of a new generation PCB engine fitting the same envelope as a Pegasus but rated at 27,000 lb dry and 40,000 lb with PCB. Clearly this is the way to go, and the author would cut almost any other defence programme to provide the funds.

Such an engine would have front nozzles delivering at 1,400°C compared with the 1,150°C of current testing on the old Pegasus 2. Hot-gas reingestion is seen as a major potential difficulty with such hot front jets, one small palliative being to toe in the front nozzles in the VTO mode to destroy the hot fountain created by the four-poster arrangement. Another problem is the larger frontal area of a boosted engine, to counter which the aircraft must be carefully area-ruled and have minimum fuselage cross-section. For a given core airflow the PCB engine lifts a larger aircraft, so RCV control bleed will be greater than with the Harrier. But these are relatively trivial difficulties, and there is thought to be no major risk attending a three-nozzle supersonic V/STOL.

In January 1981 prolonged missionary work by MCAir and Rolls-Royce surfaced with the formal proposition of a four or five-year programme costing an estimated $300-$500 million to fly at least an 11PCB, if not an 11-35PCB, in a grossly rebuilt AV-8A designated AV-8SX (for Supersonic Experimental). Though it would have to remain a four-poster aircraft the SX would have a 6-foot plug in the fuselage, long variable supersonic inlets, supersonic wing with larger flaps built on the existing wing box and many smaller changes including an up-blowing RCV at the tail. The 11F-35 engine with an airflow of 464 lb/sec (compared with 432 for a Pegasus 11) and PCB temperature of 1,527°C (2,780°F) would be rated at 33,430 lb with zero nozzle splay. Flight Mach number would be 1.6.

Beyond this demonstrator, which has had a favourable reception from the USAF as well as the Navy, NASA and British MoD, one can see a limitless series of exciting possible V/STOL fighters. Basic data for the 1989 generation appear in the Appendices, but such an aircraft could be a traditional four-poster or a three-poster with a close coupled canard. The latter appears to have the edge in manoeuvrability over anything else in the sky. Another, shown in an accompanying artist's impression, would be a larger canard with the possible advantage of being able to lift out the engine without first removing the wing.

To the impartial observer the Harrier story appears to represent to an extraordinary degree the gradual triumph of the far-sighted few against the closed and obstructive minds of the many. At the start the project was born into the incredible environment in which the view of the official establishment in Britain was that the RAF would require no more manned fighters or attack aircraft – ever. Gradually this was replaced by a NATO enthusiasm for V/STOL jets, triggered by the belated recognition than everything parked on a NATO airfield will probably be destroyed before any European war officially begins. This enthusiasm collapsed because of European nationalism at the political and industrial level, reinforced by the consistent posture of the USAF that completely overlooks the vulnerability of airfields, to the point of talking about 'taking off between the craters'! Lone voices crying in the wilderness were suddenly and unexpectedly given new strength in the spring of 1982 when the Harrier and Sea Harrier not only defeated a numerically superior enemy but provided airpower in circumstances where every other aircraft on Earth would have been unable to operate.

This is despite the fact that the aircraft that took part represented the very first generation of the Harrier family, in many respects (such as the crucial matter of EW equipment) starved of funds by successive governments so that shortcomings had to be rectified by hasty lash-ups on the spot. Thanks to the South Atlantic war the RAF and Royal Navy aircraft (not just of the Harrier family) are already being made far more battleworthy. But the next major development stage still remains cloudy and uncertain. What has become ever more obvious is that each year less and less becomes possible, and it costs more and more. PCB, for example, seemed only a short step away from supersonic V/STOL squadrons in the early 1960s. By 1980 it seemed to be several years away. Today, in the mid-1980s, it seems a decade away. The further we take the technology, the further away the end-product appears to recede. It is now coming up to a quarter-century since work began on the PCB Pegasus, and yet all Rolls-Royce can say is that current research is intended to investigate gas flow in ground effect, and to establish the standards for a still-nebulous future production engine which might be used in a next-generation aircraft (Harrier III?) some time in the 1990s.

Such aircraft get a bit remote from the title of this book, but they could never have happened without the Harrier. This aircraft, far more than any other, must be the key to military aviation's future.

Appendices

Specifications

P.1127
Span: 24ft 4in (XP984 22ft 10in)
Length: (excluding probe) 41ft 2in (XP984 42ft 0in)
Height: 10ft 9in
Wing Area: 185sq ft
Weight: (typical) 10,200lb empty; 15,500lb loaded
Engine: 11,000lb Pegasus 2 (BS.53/3)

Kestrel
Span: 22ft 10in
Length: (excluding probe) 42ft 0in
Height: 10ft 9in
Wing area: 186 sq ft
Weight: 11,000lb basic operating; 13,000lb loaded VTO; 17,000lb loaded STO; 19,000lb max loaded
Engine: 15,500lb Pegasus 5

P.1150
Span: 24ft 3in
Length: 50ft 0in (developed version 52ft 0in)
Height: 11ft 0in
Wing area: 220sq ft
Engine: 24,000lb Pegasus 5PCB (developed version 30,000lb Pegasus 6PCB)

P.1154RAF
Span: 26ft 0in
Length: 56ft 6in
Height: 12ft 3in
Wing area: 250sq ft
Weight: 18,120lb basic operating; 30,970lb loaded (lo attack mission)
Rate of climb: over 50,000ft/min
Service ceiling: 52,500ft
Level speed: Mach 1.13 (860mph) at sea level: Mach 1.93 (1,276mph) at 36,000ft
Mission radius: 308nm (355 miles) lo-hi-lo at Mach 0.93 with bomb load
Engine: 35,600lb BS.100/8

P.1145 RN
Span: 30ft 6in (developed version 36ft 0in)
Length: 58ft 6in
Height: 13ft 3in
Wing area: 287ft (developed version 350sq ft)
Weight: 24,300lb basic operating; 39,400lb loaded for intercept mission (developed version 26,000lb basic operating; 44,700lb loaded for intercept mission)
Engines: One 35,170lb BS.100/8 Phase 2 (developed version, two 18,000lb Rolls-Royce RB.168D)

Harrier GR.1
Span: 25ft 3in; 29ft 8in with ferry tips
Length: 45ft 8in
Height: 11ft 3in
Wing Area: 201sq ft; 217sq ft with ferry tips
Weight: 12,300lb basic operating; over 25,000lb max loaded
Rate of climb: 40,000ft/min; time from standing start to 40,000ft – 2min 22.7sec
Level speed: over 737mph at sea level
Mission radius: See AV-8A
Engine: 19,000lb Pegasus 6 Mk 101

Harrier T.2
Length: 55ft 9.5in
Height: 12ft 0in
Weight: 13,300lb basic operating (typical with ballast)

Harrier GR.3
Length: LRMTS
Engine: 21,500lb Pegasus 11 Mk 103

AV-8A as GR.3 except:
Weight: 12,190lb basic operating; 17,050lb max loaded VTO at 90°F; 22,300lb max loaded STO at 90°F; 25,000 design max loaded
Mission radius: (on a 90°F day with 3,000lb ordnance) 50nm from VTO; 150nm from 400ft run; 380nm from 1,200ft run; (with 5,000lb (limit) ordnance) 150nm from 1,000ft run; 250nm from 1,200ft run
Engine: Originally 20,500lb Pegasus 10 Mk 102 (figures as for Mk 103 (F402-RR-402)

Sea Harrier FRS.1
Length: 47ft 7in; 42ft 3in nose folded
Height: 12ft 2in
Weight: Not released; 8,000lb max ordnance
Time to combat: Under 6min from alarm to combat 35 miles distant
Level speed: Over 737mph at sea level
Mission radius: 460 miles hi intercept with allowance for 3min combat and VL reserves; 288 miles strike radius (load not stated)
Engine: 21,500lb Pegasus 11 Mk 104

YAV-8B
Span: 30ft 3.5in
Wing area: 230sq ft
Weight: 12,550lb basic operating; 29,750lb max design
Level speed: 674mph clean at low level; Mach 0.91 (600mph) at altitude
Range: 0.224nm/lb with five pylons and guns; 0.140nm/lb with seven Mk 82 bombs and guns
Engine: 21,500lb YF402-RR-404

AV-8B
Span: 30ft 3.5in
Length: 46ft 3.75in
Height: 11ft 8in
Wing area: 230sq ft
Weight: 12,750lb basic operating; 19,185lb max VTO at 90°F; 29,750lb max STO
Level speed: 673mph clean at low level; Mach 0.93 (615mph) at altitude; with typical attack stores at low altitude 540mph
Mission radius: 1,000ft STO at 90°F, 172 miles with 12 Mk 82 bombs and no external fuel including 60min loiter, or 748 miles with seven bombs and two tanks (no loiter); ferry range 3,310 miles
Engine: 21,180 lb F402-RR-406 (Pegasus 11-21; RAF, Pegasus 105)

Below: A model of the proposed Harrier Mk 5 with the Big Wing, with LERX, claimed to beat the AV-8B in cruising drag and aircraft manoeuvrability, besides being retrofittable on existing Harriers or Sea Harriers./*BAe*

TAV-8B as AV-8B except:
Length: 50 ft 5 in

Big Wing Harrier
Span: 32ft 0in
Wing area: 250sq ft
Level speed: Not less than Harrier GR.3; turn rate at lo level not less than 19°/sec in air-combat role
Engine: 22,200lb Pegasus 11-21E; 23,500lb Pegasus 11F-35

AV-8E as AV-8B except:
Length: probably 46ft 4in
Wing area: probably increased by Lerx
Weight: 13,800lb basic operating; 22,950lb basic flight design; 17,600lb with max useful load (7,850lb or 8,050lb internal fuel); 20,700lb VTO: 29,200lb STO with 600ft roll, 20kt WOD and 2ft sink; 31,400lb ski-jump with 390ft roll; 30,000lb rocket-assisted, zero roll.
Speed: Mach 0.91 (692mph) max with seven empty pylons
Engine: 23,200lb (guaranteed min)/23,500lb (average) Pegasus 11F-35

AV-8SX
Length: c53ft
Span: around 30ft
Weight: c15,500lb basic operating; max unlikely to exceed 30,000lb
Level speed: Mach 1.6 (1,055mph) at altitude
Range: Greater than AV-8B except when supersonic
Engine: 33,430lb Pegasus 11F-35PCB

Next generation baseline
Span: 30ft 0in
Length: 52ft 1in canard; 55ft 7in trad configuration
Height: 14ft 10in canard; 11ft 4in trad configuration
Wing Area: 300sq ft
Weight: 17,950lb basic operating; 28,450lb max VTO; c40,000lb max STO
Level speed: Supersonic, clean at low level; cMach 2 at altitude
Mission radius: Better than AV-8B
Engine: 33,430lb Pegasus 11F-35PCB

Production

P.1127 XP831, 21-10-60, Fairey controls, damaged Paris 16-6-63, at RAF Museum; XP836, 7-7-61, Dowty, lost Yeovilton 14-12-61; XP972, Pegasus 3, Fairey, damaged Tangmere 9-62; XP976, 12-7-62, kinked wing, Fairey, to 71 MU and cannibalised; XP980, -62, 12-ft tailplane 18° anhedral, Kestrel wingtip, Dowty, radio-controlled barrier trials Tarrant Rushton; XP984, Kestrel wing, Dowty, RAE.
Kestrel XS688, 7-3-64, became 64-18262; XS 689, 28-5-64, became 64-18263; XS690, 5-8-64, became 64-18264; XS691, 5-9-64, became 64-18265; XS692, 7-11-64, became 64-18266; XS693, 25-11-64, to Dunsfold though US No issued; XS694, 10-12-64, became 64-18269; XS695, 17-2-65, RAE/AAEE; XS696, 5-3-65, lost West Raynham 1-4-65. Of the six XV-6As Nos 263 and 268 were passed from AFFTC Edwards to NASA Langley.
P.1127RAF XV276, 31-8-66; XV277, 9-11-66, later Lerx/Cads; XV278, 31-12-66; XV279, 4-3-67; XV280, -4-67; XV281, -6-67.
Harrier GR.1 (survivors uprated to GR.3) XV738-743, retained for development by HSA, RR and AAEE; XV744-762, 776-810, XW630, XW763-770, 916-924, RAF inventory.
Harrier T.2 (survivors uprated as 2A and 4) XW174, 24-4-69, lost 4-6-69; XW175 completed development; XW264 (3-10-69) -272, XW925-927, 933-934 for inventory.
Harrier GR.3 includes 50 former GR.1 and 1A plus: XZ128-139, XZ963-973, XZ2987-999.
Harrier T.4 XZ145-147, XZ445, ZB600-603, RAF inventory.
Harrier T.4N ZB604-606, RN inventory.
Sea Harrier FRS.1 XZ438-440, XZ450-460, XZ491-500, ZA174-177, ZA190-195, ZD578-582 and ZD607-615.
Sea Harrier FRS.51 Six for Indian Navy (601-606) plus a further ten (607-616).
Harrier Mk 52 G-VTOL.
Harrier T.60 Four for Indian Navy (621-624).
AV-8A (Mk 50) BuAer Nos 158384-395, 158694-711, 158948-977, 159230-259, 159366-377. Survivors (61) being updated to AV-8C.
AV-8S (Mk 53) BuAer 159557-562, 161174-178.
TAV-8A (Mk 54) BuAer 159378-385.
TAV-8S (Mk 55) BuAer 159563-564.
YAV-8B BuAer 158394-395 (ex-AV-8A).
AV-8B FSD aircraft BuAer 161396-399, pilot production 161573-584, production from 162068-085 onwards.
Harrier GR.5 Harrier II for RAF, total 60, exclusive of two development aircraft ZD318-319.
TAV-8B Planned buy of 27 aircraft, not included in above totals.

Below: Artist's impression of a PCB-engined supersonic attack fighter based on configuration studies of the late 1960s. This latter-day blend of P.1154 and Harrier would have had a span of 30 feet and length of 50 feet./*BAe*